DON'T LET THE DEVIL STEAL YOUR DESTINY

DON'T LET THE DEVIL STEAL YOUR DESTINY

NORVEL HAYES

Harrison House
Tulsa, Oklahoma

Unless otherwise indicated, all Scripture quotations are taken from the *King James Version* of the Bible.

Direct quotations from the Bible appear in bold type.

Don't Let the Devil Steal Your Destiny
ISBN 1-57794-107-1
Copyright © 1998 by Norvel Hayes
P. O. Box 1379
Cleveland, Tennessee 37311

Published by Harrison House, Inc.
P. O. Box 35035
Tulsa, Oklahoma 74153

Contents

—1—

God's Way Versus the Devil's Way

God has no evil about Him. He is holy and full of love and power. He wants you to be full of that same love and power.

The Devil is in the world to torment human beings. He wants to kill, steal and destroy everything you have or ever will have. The question is: Will you let him?

You will let the Devil steal, kill and destroy in your life as long as you are ignorant of both his and God's ways.

God wants all evil that visits your life and causes you harm to leave. And He wants *you* to make it happen.

"Make it leave, Brother Norvel?" you might ask. "I don't know how to make it leave. What do you mean?"

All right, let me tell you. You can't make the Devil leave just by talking about it. Jesus said there's only one way to make the Devil leave: by using His name to cast the Devil out!

Now understand this: God's great blessings don't come cheap. If you want to know the truth about it, they're actually free. The Lord Jesus Christ Himself has already paid for them. But they don't fall on you automatically.

You must dig, seek and believe for God's great blessings. You must show God that you're willing to seek

Him for His best and that you won't stand for second best. I guarantee you, if you do that He will give you His best, because God is a great rewarder. And His greatest reward is your divine destiny in Him. God has plans for your welfare with a successful expected end. (Jer. 29:11.) So of course, the Devil seeks to steal, kill and destroy those plans.

To keep the Devil from stealing your divine destiny, you need to know the difference between his ways of operating and God's ways.

First of all, you need to know that the Devil and demons exist. Some people don't believe in demons, and many others who do are sadly ignorant about them.

Ignorance of the spirit world is the Devil's greatest weapon. Hosea 4:6 says:

My people are destroyed for lack of knowledge....

So we need to know God's Word and know what we are doing.

A full-gospel minister friend of mine has learned a lot about demons. He came out of a traditional denomination like I did. He was very well educated, too, with two doctor's degrees. And he had all of his church programs just right. Each Sunday, everything was perfectly planned and organized.

Well, a full-gospel preacher came to town and started holding tent meetings. So my friend decided to attend a few sessions, you know, to see what they were like.

One night, as my pastor friend sat in the service, the preacher was praying for people and was confronted by a demon-possessed person. As this preacher laid hands on the man, he growled, jerked loose and ran to where my friend was seated.

Then this demon-possessed man stuck his finger in my friend's face and said, "Ha, ha, ha, ha, ha! I am the demon over your church doctrines and I planned your service last Sunday! Ha, ha, ha, ha, ha!"

This pastor thought he and the church deacons had planned the service. He told me later, "I knew somebody planned it, but I didn't know that demons did. I only knew that God wasn't doing anything in my services. They were cold, dry and dead. And I knew God didn't make them that way."

So my friend started digging in the Scriptures trying to find the truth about how he could get more of God's power in his church. And eventually he learned about the baptism in the Holy Spirit.

My friend was not alone. The whole church of Jesus Christ has missed it by depending on programs instead of on God's Word and the power of the Holy Spirit.

I have no problem believing that the Devil did plan my friend's Sunday service, because half of his congregation sat there every week broke and sick.

God doesn't make people broke and sick. That's not His will. He sent His Son Jesus to earth so you could have heaven upon you.

Heaven has nothing to do with failure. Heaven has no control over the parts of your life that aren't successful. Failure is the Devil's way. It is the work of hell.

If you are failing in some way, my brother, you're allowing demons you don't even recognize to operate in that failing area of your life. And you need to spiritually

9

inventory yourself from the top of your head to the bottom of your feet. Inventory your life, your business, your pocketbook. Count your money. Are you doing things God's way?

Take an Inventory

Take inventory of your love. Do you have it or not? You need to walk in God's kind of love to find His destiny for you and to prosper in this life.

"Well, Brother Norvel," you say, "I love some people. But I think you ought to hang that sinning preacher at daybreak."

If you can say that, you don't have God's love working in you. And unless you change your attitude, you never will.

God instructs us to pray for our brothers and sisters who are caught in sin.

If any man see his brother sin a sin which is not unto death, he shall ask, and he shall give him life for them that sin not unto death.... All unrighteousness is sin: and there is a sin not unto death.
1 John 5:16,17

And God forgives those who confess their sins to Him and repent.

If we confess our sins, he is faithful and just to forgive us our sins, and to cleanse us from all unrighteousness.
1 John 1:9

If you're quick to criticize a member of the family of God, you'll have to struggle through life doing the best you can. You'll have to find a little house and pray to God that you will have enough money to pay your bills. Some months you will, and some you won't.

"I don't know why I can't ever get ahead, Brother Norvel," you say. "I love the Lord, and I go to church...a charismatic church! I even dance before the Lord!"

Is that right? Well, if you do go to a charismatic church and dance before the Lord, your mind is probably as loose as your body. You have to think like God thinks if you want Him to bless you. He doesn't bless loose minds. Get chapter and verse from Scripture for what you believe and don't ever change.

Your neighbors and the people you work with in the ministry might change. But God's Word and His love have never changed — and they never will.

For God so loved the world, that he gave his only begotten Son, that whosoever believeth in him should not perish, but have everlasting life.

John 3:16

John tells us the way it is. The everlasting destiny of God is fulfilled in *whosoever* believeth in Jesus.

You may have had ten spouses and been an alcoholic for forty years. You may be a successful businessman who has been in bed with every prostitute in town. It doesn't matter. God loves you and wants to save you.

"Well Brother Norvel," you say, "I'm too mean for God. I'm too disgusting for Him."

No, you're not, my sister. You're disgusting all right, but you're not too disgusting for Him.

God is so powerful that He can wipe that sin out of you, wash you as white as snow and make you a brand new person — totally new. He can roll the burden of that old sin away and make you feel like an angel, glory to God.

11

Jesus will set you on a mountaintop full of joy, peace and compassion if you'll let Him. There is nothing He won't do for you. He paid the price for your sins. And He wants you to receive the full benefits of His sacrifice on the cross.

The Power in God's Love

God's love is powerful enough to overcome any sin and lead any sinner into their divine destiny in a rich life of success. His power can change lives.

A member of our church in Cleveland, Tennessee, used to be totally demon-possessed. At one time she was ready to jump off the top of a twenty-five-story building and kill herself. Back then she hated the world and everything in it, especially the human race.

Now this sweet woman carries a Bible everywhere she goes. She's so full of God's love that she loves everything and everybody. She lives to testify for Jesus and do whatever God wants her to do. She overcomes the Devil by the blood of the Lamb and by the word of her testimony. And that's how we are to overcome, too.

And they overcame him by the blood of the Lamb, and by the word of their testimony....
Revelation 12:11

You need God's power to have victory over the Devil. You either have that power or you don't. There is no in-between. God says the Holy Spirit living inside of you is greater than the Devil that is in the world. And you need to know that the Devil doesn't want you to know it.

Ye are of God, little children, and have overcome them: because greater is he that is in you, than he that is in the world.
1 John 4:4

God's Way Is Prosperity

To achieve God's divine destiny for your life, you also need to know that He wants to prosper you. But He wants you to prosper *His* way.

The blessing of the Lord, it maketh rich, and he addeth no sorrow with it.

Proverbs 10:22

Some time ago, I had an opportunity in just one business deal to make a million dollars cash. I have lots of opportunities like that.

"Well, Brother Norvel," you say, "I guess you took that opportunity, didn't you?"

No, I didn't.

Why?

Because I don't want the money. God delivered me years ago from lusting after money. So passing up a big financial deal doesn't bother me.

Besides, I'm already rich. I've been a *multi-millionaire* for years. Being just a *millionaire* is kind of low-level to me.

I don't even receive a salary from my ministry. Nearly every offering received in the church at our Bible School in Tennessee goes to build and run a home for unwed mothers, or for the Bible School or another part of our ministry.

I can remember once when some guest speakers at one of my meetings took up a love offering for me. I think I have personally received maybe three or four offerings over the past eight years.

But when people give to our ministry, we ask them where they want their money to go — to the unwed mothers' home, the Bible School or some other area.

Then we put their contribution in that account. I don't take it, I guarantee you. [The million dollar deal I was telling you about was an offer on my ministry property].

I could have sold our ministry property in Tennessee for a million dollars. But I want to use that place for the Lord, to win souls and bless people. I don't want to sell it.

God told me supernaturally how to get that property and I'm not going to sell Him out. I told Him if He ever wanted me to sell that property, I would duplicate it for Him and His glory.

Secrets to Financial Success

I can teach you in just a few minutes how to have God's blessings fall on you. Would you like to know why I'm successful financially? I'm successful because I worship God and help people.

If you'll worship God, help other people and cast out devils in Jesus' name, then God will abundantly bless you.

I know exactly why the blessing of God fell on me. I know when it came and why it stays. And God will do the same for you. I don't have an exclusive right to His blessings. What He does for me, He will also do for you.

Remember them which have the rule over you, who have spoken unto you the word of God: whose faith follow, considering the end of their conversation. Jesus Christ the same yesterday, and to day, and for ever.

Hebrews 13:7,8

...God is no respecter of persons: But in every nation he that feareth him, and worketh righteousness, is accepted with him.

Acts 10:34,35

"But Brother Norvel," you say, "God's not blessing me like He's blessing you!"

Well, it's your own dumb fault. And it really is dumb, too. It's dumb to be broke when you can have anything you want. It's stupid to be sick when you can be healthy.

Secrets to Prosperity

Again, learn to worship God. You need to learn to love Him, love your neighbor as yourself and use Jesus' name to exercise the authority God gave you over the Devil. When you do these things, God will bless and prosper you the way He does me.

From the natural standpoint, I admit that I have always been a good, hard worker. For years, I put in twelve, fifteen or even eighteen hours a day to make my business a success.

God doesn't like lazy people. God blesses people who work. He loves them, but He doesn't like them, because He can't bless them.

Go to the ant, thou sluggard; consider her ways, and be wise: Which having no guide, overseer, or ruler, provideth her meat in the summer, and gathereth her food in the harvest.

Proverbs 6:6-8

God doesn't like laziness, my brother. He doesn't like anything that keeps Him from blessing you, my sister.

So, being a hard worker, I was in pretty good shape to receive God's blessing. But I still put my business before God. Even though I had started to teach the Bible, I wasn't allowing Him to be Lord of my life.

15

I had a lot of business sense. I built my company up to where my salary was as much as six thousand dollars a week. I made more than the governor of my state and most other people in my generation.

I was like most other human beings, though. We humans start businesses, drive luxury cars, buy a half-dozen homes and fill our bank accounts. And because we can do this, we think we're smart.

But when I met God, I found out that He sees six thousand dollars a week as nothing. I found out that I was broke and didn't know it.

"Why don't you get involved with Me?" the Lord asked. "Make Me your business partner. Stop putting your business before Me."

I said, "Oh, uh, well, uh...." That's what too many of us say when God asks us a question.

If you want to know the truth about the matter, no one ever finds out how really dumb they are until God talks to them. When He tells you what He thinks, you wonder how you ever had enough sense to come in out of the rain.

So, I got real smart, put God ahead of my business and made Jesus my business partner. And God has prospered me abundantly since.

God wants to be Lord over your life *now*. He doesn't want you to put anything else ahead of Him.

Worship Is Vital in Fulfilling Your Destiny

After walking with the Lord for a number of years and working for Him, I thought I was in pretty good shape.

Then God brought me up short. Something in my life was keeping me from moving on in His destiny for me.

If you understand what I'm about to share with you, and apply it in your life, it will help you.

One day, the word of the Lord came to me saying, "Son, the church is sadly lacking."

"Sadly lacking in what, Lord?" I asked, because I didn't know.

"The church is sadly lacking. They don't worship Me enough. I'm God. I want to be worshiped. They don't worship Me enough, and neither do you. I want you to start teaching churches to worship Me. And you start worshiping Me more yourself."

Then He told me what He would do when His people started to worship Him faithfully.

"When I look down," the Lord said, "and I see everyone in a local church — or an individual person in private — worshiping Me, lifting up holy hands, making Me their God, it gets My attention. Then and only then do I become God to them."

In other words, as God sits on His throne and you bow down and begin to worship Him sincerely, He looks your way. It is then that He begins to work for you to give you everything you want. Not *need*. *Want*.

The Lord said He would do that for anyone who worshiped Him. So until you learn to worship God, you won't walk in the fullness of His destiny for you.

You can choose a career. Then you can go to college and learn how to do the work you've chosen. It takes six to eight years to become a doctor, and three or four years to be an accountant. How long you spend in school depends on the occupation you're pursuing.

Then after you graduate, you can work hard and achieve what the world calls success. You can have two cars, a pretty wife or handsome husband, a child, a dog and a few thousand dollars a week coming in.

You might even work your way up the world's ladder of success to where you earn fourteen million dollars a year. The world calls that successful, but God doesn't.

Why?

Because if you don't bow down before God and worship Him, you're not successful in God's eyes, and you never will be.

God doesn't measure your success by how much money you have. He measures it by how much you love Him.

Worshiping God When Alone

When thou prayest, enter into thy closet, and when thou hast shut thy door, pray to thy Father which is in secret; and thy Father which seeth in secret shall reward thee openly.

Matthew 6:6

From the day God talked to me about worshiping Him, I started spending time doing that.

Now, you may not be ready for my next point. You might get mad. But here it is anyway.

If you only worship God in church, He will not allow His great and mighty blessings and the fulness of His destiny into your life.

He will allow a certain number of blessings to come upon you. But if you don't worship Him when you are alone with Him, He will only bless you to a small degree compared with what He would like to do.

So let me say it again — to receive God's greatest blessings, you have to worship Him when you are alone, by yourself.

...and thy Father which seeth in secret shall reward thee openly.

God says He will reward you openly for what He sees you do in secret. How will He reward you? He will give you wisdom, love, knowledge, compassion, money, help, joy, peace...*everything!*

God doesn't work part-time, and He doesn't leave things out. He is the Author of life, my brother. He knows exactly what you need to live a fulfilled life, my sister.

This also is true for a local church. If an entire congregation learns to worship Him, He will bless that church.

The denomination doesn't matter. If the members of that group are born again by God's Spirit, He will bless them mightily as they worship Him. And that local church will be successful.

God's Prosperity Includes Peace

Here is another area where God's idea of prosperity is different from the world's idea.

You can have all of the world's wisdom, and all the money, and still not be happy. You can go to church and do good works for God. But if you don't have God's wisdom and His peace that passes understanding in your mind, you will never be successful or prosperous.

If someone offered me twenty-five million dollars in a tub and said, "Norvel, take it and the spirit of confusion that comes with it — just live with it a few years," I'd say, "Oh no. Nooooo. Uh-uh."

I wouldn't trade the peace of God for all the money in the world.

Why?

Because I know what it's like not to have that peace.

Some people are ashamed to give their testimony, but I'm not. That's one reason God blesses me so much. For more than a year after my first wife divorced me, I begged God to let me die. I'd go to bed at night and plead with Him to let my eyes close and never open again.

Finally, as I followed God and sought His divine destiny for me, He took that pain away and gave me His peace.

So you keep the money.... I'll keep God's peace.

No Emotional Valleys

Why be confused when you can have a clear mind? Why be sad and lonely when you can be full of joy and have God's power surging through your body all the time?

You don't need emotional valleys. And if you want to know the truth about it, God doesn't believe in bad days.

"But I have some bad days, Brother Norvel," you say. "Some days I'm up and some days I'm down. Don't you have days like that too, Brother Norvel?"

No! I don't! All of my days are full of joy, peace, contentment and success. *All* of them. And as long as I say that, they always will be. Jesus said to say it is so.

Verily I say unto you, That *whosoever* shall say unto this mountain, Be thou removed, and be thou cast into the sea; and shall not doubt in his heart, but shall believe that those things which he

20

saith shall come to pass; he shall have whatsoever he saith.

Mark 11:23

In this Scripture, Jesus explains that every person on earth will have whatever he or she says. Every time God wanted to create something in Genesis 1, He spoke. Scripture says, **And God said....**

And God made us with that same ability. We create with our words. So let's make sure that we are creating good things in our lives.

If you're saying nothing, or the wrong things, then you're in a mess. And if you don't open your mouth and start saying what God has told you to say, you'll be in a bigger mess.

Make up your mind to change what you say to agree with what God says.

Learn to Cast Out Devils

If you want to walk in the fulness of God's destiny for you, you are also going to need to know how to cast out devils. The ministry of casting out devils may not be important to some people, but it is to God. Devils rage upon people's lives trying to wreck them, *and God doesn't like it!*

God doesn't want you listening to devils so they can wreck your life. You're made in His image and He loves you.

If you know right from wrong, then you know about devils. Right and good things come into your life from God. Evil, mean and harmful things come into your life from the Devil. It's not complicated.

So when any evil, mean or harmful thing tries to come into your life, rise up and say, "In Jesus' name, *no!* You will *not* come into my life!"

The greatest word you can ever say to a devil is, "No!"

Why?

Because the Devil and his servants are always trying to get us to do something evil, mean or harmful.

Someone will ask, "Have you ever tried marijuana? No? Here! Just smoke this! It will send you on an unusual trip!"

Right. Some of my buddies tried that stuff and they were on a trip for thirty years!

Just say, "No! I'm not trying drugs! I don't have to have them. I belong to Jesus!"

Maybe the Devil will tempt you with alcoholic beverages.

"Oh," someone may say to you, "doesn't this whiskey look good! Pour it over some ice."

Just say *"No!* I will *not* drink whiskey. I drink Seven-Up! It's caffeine-free!"

You have to watch yourself.

The Devil might tempt you with someone from the opposite sex.

If you're a woman, a girlfriend might say, "Ohhh, girl! Look at that guy! Doesn't he look good?"

He may be the most unstable, unreliable, irresponsible man who ever put on a pair of pants. And if you get involved with him you'll learn that, but you might learn too late.

It works the same way if you're a man. That woman might look good. But she might be the biggest pain in the neck you've ever had the misfortune to meet. And you might not find that out until after you're married.

So if you're single and you want a spouse, bow down before God and worship Him. Trust Him to send you the right mate in His timing.

Don't ever lust after marriage. If you do, you'll never get God's will. Marriage is one of the most important steps you will ever take in your life. And God doesn't fulfill lust. He only fulfills faith exercised with patience.

You'd better make a note of that. Write it down, or the Devil will make sure that you forget it. It could save you twenty-five years of heartache, and possibly your life.

Jesus doesn't fulfill lust! Did you get that? When you have faith in Him, and you exercise that faith with patience, He will bless you with great blessings and fulfill your destiny.

Lust is one of the Devil's most common ways of stealing a believer's destiny, and you need to know that. The Devil works with all kinds of lust. If he can trick you into lusting after something, he can get you out of God's will. But you don't have to fall for his trickery.

When you learn to exercise faith with patience, and walk in God's love, you learn to walk in the Spirit. And when you walk in the Spirit, you will not fulfill the lust of the flesh.

As a Christian, you don't have to yield to lust.

This I say then, Walk in the Spirit, and ye shall not fulfil the lust of the flesh.

Galatians 5:16

What you lust for looks so attractive. The way it works reminds me of a butterfly.

The butterfly is one of God's most graceful creatures. It floats through the air looking so colorful and beautiful. As it passes by, you just want to reach out and catch it.

But when you do catch that butterfly and open up your hand to look at it...ugh!

That's how lust looks after you fulfill it.

My flesh lusts. Oh that's right, just like your flesh lusts. It wants what it wants *now*. My flesh today has no respect for the condition of my mind tomorrow. So Jesus gives us a way of escape.

> **There hath no temptation taken you but such as is common to man: but God is faithful, who will not suffer you to be tempted above that ye are able; but will with the temptation also make a way to escape, that ye may be able to bear it.**
>
> **1 Corinthians 10:13**

But when you're not walking in the Spirit and you fulfill lust, you commit sin. And by doing that, you separate yourself from God and crumble the foundation of your faith.

The day after you sin, if somebody asks you, "Do you have faith in God?" you won't reply, "Glory to God! *Yes!*" You'll say, "I don't know. I guess so."

So God gives a way to start over again. God allows us to confess our sin and to repent. Scripture says,

> **If we confess our sins, he is faithful and just to forgive us our sins, and to cleanse us from all unrighteousness.**
>
> **1 John 1:9**

Thank God, Jesus is in the people-restoring business!

The Devil Works With Lust

So remember, if you start wanting to be married so much that you can hardly stand it, repent before God. Because if you lust after marriage, the Devil will send you a mate.

Don't get in a hurry. You have time.

The Devil tells people in their twenties that they'd better hurry up and get married because they're getting old. A devil will whisper in their ear, "Half of your schoolmates are married. Why aren't you? There must be something wrong with you."

If you don't cast down those thoughts in Jesus' name, that devil will have you ready to marry the first person who comes along; especially a good-looking one. And when the devil moves in to live with you in him or her, he will fight hard against your destiny.

Now, at first a marriage may *look* like God was in it. Things might start out kind of sweet. But after six months or so a day will come when he or she won't look nearly as wonderful as you thought. Reality will hit and you'll look at yourself in the mirror and say, "How did I ever get involved with this guy? Where did I ever find this girl? This isn't a marriage. I am in total bondage."

Marriage Is Not Bondage

Marriage is not bondage. If you're in a marriage filled with bondage, then you're in a mess.

Now, I'm not saying to be unfaithful. Be a faithful mate. And I'm not saying that give-and-take isn't needed in a marriage. Do all you can to cooperate and love your mate. What I am saying is, marriage is not bondage and you are never to be under your mate's total control.

Let's say you want to go to the store and your husband says, "I don't want you to go. I'll bet you'll talk to some guy. Who did you talk to the last time you went to the store?" If that happens, tell him to shut his mouth and bring him to one of my services. I'll cast the evil spirit of jealousy out of him. If you don't do that, you'll have to live with that spirit of jealousy for years. It won't leave on its own.

So if your mate starts getting messed up in his or her thinking, get the devil cast out so you can live in peace. If you want to go to the grocery store, you shouldn't have to ask your husband. If you go along with that way of life, you're as crazy as he is. Doesn't he trust you? That kind of relationship is bondage, and God hates everything about it.

Jealousy in the Church

Some pastors give place to a jealous spirit in their churches.

"I am the pastor of this church," they might say, "and I'm protecting my sheep! So I won't announce the meeting at that full gospel church down the street. Some of my members might go and never come back! These are *my* sheep!"

Now, of course pastors are supposed to protect the sheep. That's part of their job. But they need to remember that the church and its members belong to God, not to them. So if your pastor refuses to let "his" members attend special services at other churches of like precious faith, then leave. Go to that other church and never come back.

God didn't call you to be part of a church under some jealous pastor who is keeping his congregation in bondage.

Churches of the Lord Jesus Christ are supposed to cooperate and love each other. So if you want to go visit another Pentecostal church having a special meeting where you can be fed on God's Word, then go, glory to God. Life is too short for you to spend it as a nervous wreck because you think your pastor might see you go to another church. Don't get involved in that. Bring your pastor to one of my services and I'll cast the devil out of him.

"How would you do that, Brother Norvel?" you ask. "What would you say?"

I'd say, "You binding, controlling spirit: *come out of him* in Jesus' name!"

God isn't a God of bondage, my friend. He is a God of liberty and freedom. The following scriptures prove my point:

Where the Spirit of the Lord is, there is liberty.
2 Corinthians 3:17

The creature [creation] itself also shall be delivered from the bondage of corruption into the glorious liberty of the children of God.
Romans 8:21

Brethren, ye have been called unto liberty; only use not liberty for an occasion to the flesh, but by love serve one another.
Galatians 5:13

Remember, God doesn't fulfill lust; the Devil does. Do you want money so much that you would do anything for it? If so, I guarantee you that the Devil will provide some small, illegal way for you to make a whole lot of money. The Devil will set a trap and you'll fall into it.

Faith With Patience

God fulfills faith. He doesn't honor nervous faith. He wants you to develop faithful patience to become "perfect" (mature) as James says:

My brethren, count it all joy when ye fall into divers temptations; knowing this, that the trying of your faith worketh patience. But let patience have her perfect work, that ye may be perfect and entire, wanting nothing.

James 1:2-4

In these verses, God says if I have faith and patience, I will end up wanting, or lacking, nothing. That's God's way. That's what He wants for us. Think about that. God is saying here that if I believe Him and His promises, and if I wait patiently for Him to fulfill those promises, then I'll end up lacking nothing. And that's true because if I want, or lack, *nothing,* then I have *everything.* To want nothing means to have everything.

Freedom of Choice

Another of God's ways that directs us toward our destiny is the freedom of choice. Joshua understood this during Israel's glory days.

If it seem evil unto you to serve the Lord, choose you this day whom ye will serve....

Joshua 24:15

But Satan blinds people's minds so they don't know they have a choice and so they will choose the wrong things. As Paul writes:

If our gospel be hid, it is hid to them that are lost: In whom the god of this world hath blinded the minds of them which believe not, lest the light of the glorious gospel of Christ, who is the image of God, should shine unto them.

2 Corinthians 4:3,4

This blinding plot of Satan is why it is so important for Christians to accept all kinds of people into the church. When you get a person away from a demon-dominated atmosphere and into one dominated by the Spirit of God, that person will recognize the wrong they've been doing, and wake up to their destiny in Christ. This is why Jesus said, **Go out into the highways and hedges, and compel them to come in, that my house may be filled** (Luke 14:23).

Compel Them

If you are a Christian fulfilling your divine destiny, you will be bringing people into the house of the Lord. You will be compelling them to come in, because they don't know they're going to hell. The house and atmosphere they live in and the friends they have may seem okay to them. But they've created a lifestyle of their own.

So when unbelievers come into God's house, the Christians there need to sing songs about Jesus, love each other and praise and worship the Lord. They need to tell the story of Jesus and how much He loves everyone. Unbelievers need to hear what Jesus did to free them from the Devil's clutches. As unbelievers sit in *that* atmosphere, their hearts will start to race and the Holy Spirit can work on them.

God loves His holy sanctuaries. Great things are happening in churches by God's mighty power! We are so blessed! And as we enjoy God's blessings for the church, we need to remember that the blood of Jesus and the name of Jesus are more powerful than anything the Devil can bring against people.

Why Put Up With the Devil?

In whom we have redemption through his blood, the forgiveness of sins, according to the riches of his grace.

Ephesians 1:7

When people are born again by the Spirit of God, the blood of Jesus is applied to their lives and their sins are forgiven. And, *all* power is in Jesus' name!

Wherefore God also hath highly exalted him [Jesus], and given him a name which is above every name: That at the name of Jesus every knee should bow, of things in heaven, and things in earth, and things under the earth.

Philippians 2:9,10

So if you as a believer know what the blood of Jesus does, and the power in Jesus' name, then why do you allow devils to mess with you or your family the way you do? They have no right to dominate you. If you are putting up with disease, you are putting up with devils. Diseases are a work of hell. Some of the best-hidden devils are those that cause human disease.

"Oh, Brother Norvel," you say, "I love the Lord. I don't have any devils. I just have cancer."

Well, where do you think that cancer came from? Cancer and other diseases are sent from hell, not from heaven. Disease is the Devil's way; health, giving good gifts, is God's way. The Bible plainly tells you this.

Every good gift and every perfect gift is from above, and cometh down from the Father of lights, with whom is no variableness, neither shadow of turning.

James 1:17

This Scripture says all good things that come to you are from God, the Father of lights. So, where do you think all bad things come from? They come from the father of darkness: the Devil.

Do you think cancer is a good thing? I hope not. If anything bad is coming into your life, especially something that's trying to kill you, you need to know the Devil is behind it. Jesus said He is a murderer and a thief.

The thief cometh not, but for to steal, and to kill, and to destroy: I am come that they might have life, and that they might have it more abundantly.

John 10:10

You need to know this, my brother. You need to know this, my sister. It doesn't matter who you are, where you came from or what church you go to. Are you born again by God's Spirit? Do you know without a doubt that Jesus' blood has washed you clean from sin? Do you know the power in Jesus' name? If you can answer "yes" to these questions, then you don't have to put up with disease or devils.

The Devil is out to steal from you in every area of your life. He's out to destroy you and everything you have. So don't start wallowing around in the mud with him when he challenges your destiny. Don't put up with the Devil's ways of affliction or depression or anything else that's not the peaceful way of God. God wants people to be whole and full of the Holy Ghost. He wants them to feel as if they could run like jackrabbits.

A lot of people don't understand how much God loves them. But all they would have to do is read the following Scriptures and they'd change their thinking fast.

For God so loved the world, that he gave his only begotten Son, that whosoever believeth in him should not perish, but have everlasting life.

John 3:16

Herein is love, not that we loved God, but that he loved us, and sent his Son to be the propitiation [the one who paid the penalty] **for our sins.**

1 John 4:10

Behold, what manner of love the Father hath bestowed upon us, that we should be called the sons of God....

1 John 3:1

God's way of doing and being is so wonderful and precious. He never had sickness, poverty or any of the other awful things we go through in this life in mind for us when He created the human race. Christian, *believe* what I am telling you. God created man in His own image — His own likeness — and put him in His beautiful, bountiful garden. His destiny for the man and woman He created was fellowship, dominion and peace forever.

32

And God blessed them, and God said unto them, Be fruitful, and multiply, and replenish the earth, and subdue it: and have dominion over the fish of the sea, and over the fowl of the air, and over every living thing that moveth upon the earth.

Genesis 1:28

But the Devil messed that up. He talked the first man and woman into disobeying God and stole the great destiny God had for them. And the Devil is still trying to talk the human race into messing up. He wants to steal God's destiny for you.

Think about this now as you move on to Chapter 2. You don't have to listen to the Devil and let him steal your God-given destiny. You can take authority over the Devil in Jesus' name and walk in God's destiny for you! In the next chapter, I'm going to show you that your ministry is your destiny, and that God has one specifically designed for you.

—2—

What It Takes To Have a Ministry

God has a ministry for every believer, not just for a chosen few. He anoints each believer to do something for Him. Then He gives the believer authority and power to keep the Devil from stealing that ministry.

But what does it take for a person to actually find the ministry God has for him and fulfill that divine destiny as God intends?

First, you have to prove to God that you are sincere. You have to prove to Him that you will not be led by men but that you are open to the Holy Spirit and what He wants.

Second, you have to show God that you are willing to be His servant.

Third, you will have to get so strongly established in God's Word that you will never be influenced or led by personalities or by people with great talents. The Bible says, **For as many as are led by the Spirit of God, they are the sons of God** (Romans 8:14). God didn't call you to be led by men or women with great talents, great speaking abilities or great ministries.

"Beyond-the-Ordinary" Ministry

Romans 8:14 is talking about daughters of God, too! For example, a young woman who used to help us in our work for the Lord had an anointed public ministry of her own. Other women often told me, "She blessed me so much! I tell you, Brother Norvel, she's a blessing!"

The truth of the matter is this woman was that way all the time. Blessing people was a way of life for her. She blessed everything that moved! She held teaching seminars around the country. And she didn't receive her ministry because she traveled with Brother Norvel. I hope our ministry was a blessing to her and that she gained spiritual strength from it. But Jesus is the One Who molded her and gave her the gifts of the Spirit.

Remember, ministers are human beings just like everybody else. So don't ever follow somebody around just because he blesses you. God wants to mold *you* so you can be a blessing to others.

"Do you mean God is going to give *me* a ministry, Brother Norvel?"

Yes, He is, because you have a destiny to fulfill. All you have to do is pay the price to receive that ministry.

Everybody pays a different kind of price in order to walk in God's calling. For instance, that young woman who blessed people so much was a college graduate from West Virginia. She was a straight-A high school student who had won a scholarship to college, where she continued to make straight A's. Her IQ and grades were so high that she won the honor of traveling to Washington, D.C., to meet with the First Lady at the White House.

With her four-year college degree, this young woman could have stepped right into a good job with a big salary. She could have bought a little car and rented a comfortable apartment like so many other college graduates do. She could have remained a nice sweet girl who married some nice young man, had three or four children and lived a nice American life.

But Jesus touched this woman's life and called her to a "beyond-the-ordinary" ministry. And she just plain decided to give herself to God. She walked away from the life she could have had and ministered on the streets for two years with a youth group. She witnessed for the Lord and helped teenagers get off of drugs. She slept in tents and other people's homes and ate out of bean cans. Then, after less than six months of serving on the streets, the gifts of the Holy Spirit began to manifest through her. Many people live and die and never see the gifts of the Spirit work through them!

If you work with beaten-down, brokenhearted humanity, you will need the gifts of the Spirit. When you're helping teenagers to stop taking drugs or ministering like that to other people, the Holy Ghost will start flowing through you. He will give you His particular gift to fit each need.

Ministry Ingredients from James

There are some ingredients you will need to add to your life, if you are going to see your ministry come forth. You must make up your mind to do whatever is necessary to add them to your life. And we find these ingredients in James.

By the time we get through with James, you may feel like you've had a workout! I love that book. If people would listen to James, they would get established in their spiritual walk. They would become so strong that they wouldn't be pushed around by every wind of doctrine.

It's important that *you* develop the Bible's promise of spiritual strength. So when you go to a meeting — and I don't care what minister is speaking, even Norvel Hayes — take your Bible. Check up on what's being said. You aren't obligated to believe everything anybody tells you, no matter who they are. Don't ever let personalities influence you. Instead, make sure that what you accept is based on God's Word. If you don't, you'll get into trouble.

When you were saved and filled with the Holy Spirit, you didn't become some man's puppet. God didn't call you to follow men or personalities; He called you to follow *Him.* He wants to mold you, my friend, into what *He* wants you to be.

Now, most ministers would like to help you, and they don't want you to become their puppet. But, if you're not careful, you can get your eyes on a minister's talent or ability and mess yourself up by expecting more from him than he can give. Ministers are human, and they make a lot of mistakes.

Personally, I don't put any minister on a pedestal. Every one I've ministered with has made mistakes at one time or another. And if you hang around me long enough, you'll find out that I'm not perfect.

It is only the One Who wants to help you fulfill your divine destiny Who *is* perfect. I can't bring forth your ministry and mold you into what you really need to be, but Jesus can. I don't know all the talent within you that God wants to pull out and use for His glory. But Jesus knows exactly what you can be if you will yield yourself to Him as a servant.

So here is James' first essential ingredient to fulfilling your ministry: servanthood.

James, *a servant of God* and of the Lord Jesus Christ, to the twelve tribes which are scattered abroad, greeting.

James 1:1

You have to be willing to be a servant of God and of the Lord Jesus Christ in the ministry of your destiny. Being a servant may mean serving life to brokenhearted people, drug-addicted teenagers or broken families who feel no one can help. It may mean sharing your food with the hungry. Regardless of the need at hand, you have to show God that whatever it costs, you are willing to be His servant to bless the human race.

I know two brothers who are good examples of servanthood in ministry. For years, the oldest brother had the ministry of hitchhiking. (Now, you may laugh at that, but if God calls *you* to do it, you won't laugh anymore. You'll go out on the highways with your thumb stuck out!)

Christians sometimes pick up hitchhikers so they can witness to them. But this man was a born-again, Spirit-filled hitchhiker looking for people to pick *him* up so *he* could witness to *them*. Whoever picked him up always heard the gospel message.

For two-and-a-half years, this man hitchhiked the roads of America. He just took whatever road God wanted him to take, sticking his thumb out until somebody stopped and picked him up. He later became an intercessor at John Osteen's church in Lakewood, Texas, and his younger brother began to help with the shipping of Rev. Osteen's tapes and books.

These two brothers are servants of the Lord. A few years ago, when I went to speak at that church, the younger brother picked me up at the airport and took me to a house on the church grounds. He carried my suitcases in, helped me in any way he could, and then left.

A little while later, somebody knocked on the door. When I opened it, this same young man was standing there.

"I love you, Brother Norvel," he said. "God told me to give you this." Then he handed me twenty dollars and just turned around and walked off.

When I closed the door, the Spirit of the Lord started blessing me tremendously because of that young man. The Lord let me know that the servanthood this younger brother showed toward me was his ministry. "He's a good servant of Mine, son," Jesus told me.

You see, when you're willing to be a servant of God, you find out what living is all about.

Let me tell you about the ministry of another man, who later became a part of our ministry team. This man was a missionary from Greece to the United States. (Don't laugh — the United States has a need for missionaries just like any other country!)

When the man arrived in America, God began to use him as a witness. He attended our Bible school. Then, after graduating, he became the head of our book and tape ministry on the road.

This man has the heart of a servant. His greatest desire is to train people to witness on the streets. That's the ministry God gave him.

Some people say, "I'm not a servant of the Lord. I'm a king and a priest in Christ."

To them I say, yes, you *are* a king and a priest in Christ Jesus. But never forget that God put you in that place of authority. And you will never walk in the fullness of your authority unless you are also a servant. You must also expect to remain a servant for the rest of your life.

The word *servant* means to serve whoever needs help. That's the kind of servant God wants you to be.

I don't care how big your ministry becomes, how much faith you have or how much money is in your bank account. I don't care if you give ten million dollars a month to the gospel. You still can't escape your responsibility to reach out and help the brokenhearted. If you run from that responsibility, your ministry will never be worth much because God won't honor it.

I'm talking about finding your ministry and letting God mold you into what He wants you to be. Look at how Paul began these three New Testament letters:

Paul, a servant of Jesus Christ....

Romans 1:1

Paul and Timotheus, the servants of Jesus Christ....
Philippians 1:1

Paul, a servant of God....

Titus 1:1

The apostle Paul also wrote about Jesus' example of servanthood in the Book of Philippians.

Let this mind [attitude] be in you, which was also in Christ Jesus: Who, being in the form of God, thought it not robbery to be equal with

God: But made himself of no reputation, and took upon him the form of a servant....

Philippians 2:5-7

The Servant's Heart

My heart goes out to people who have a true servant's heart. They have such a hunger to serve Jesus that they are willing to do anything for Him. They go anywhere for Jesus, and consider it a great joy and privilege to do so. I've been around a lot of human beings in my time, and I can tell you that Jesus will give special gifts to this kind of person.

It's so sad to see people who want to serve God but are prevented from doing it. For example, one time when I was holding a series of meetings in a church in San Antonio, Texas, the pastor asked me to speak to a young woman. And I'm telling you, I don't know when I have ever met a person who wanted so much to do something for God. This woman loved Jesus with all her heart. I asked her what talents she had, and she told me that she played viola professionally for the city symphony orchestra.

"The Lord gave that talent to me," she said. "And I know the Lord wants me to give all of my talent back to Him."

Then she asked me to pray for her and to speak to her husband. "When somebody doesn't have the same calling as you do," she said, "it's hard sometimes for him to understand."

So I prayed for her. Later I also met with her husband. I just talked to him in my own easy way about his wife having the call of God on her. I told him that Jesus wanted his wife to give her musical talent to Him, and that she was willing.

"It's so important to Jesus and to her that she be able to do that," I said. "And since you walked down the aisle with her and said, 'I do,' her calling has become a part of your life, too."

If you're single, think about this when you're looking for a mate. Make sure you both have compatible callings so you can fulfill your God-given destinies together.

I'm warning you, if you become romantically involved with the wrong person, you can really mess up your life. I can't say it enough — before you become involved with anyone, talk to God.

Count It All Joy as You Learn Patience

Now let's look at another ingredient you must have to come into the fullness of God's destiny for you: joy.

My brethren, *count it all joy* when ye fall into divers temptations.

James 1:2

No matter how the Devil visits you, count it all joy.

Do you want to know what it takes to have a ministry? Joy. And let me warn you: don't ever lose it. Why? Because **the joy of the Lord is your strength** (Nehemiah 8:10).

There is joy in the presence of the Lord. David wrote, **Thou wilt shew me the path of life: in thy presence is fulness of joy; at thy right hand there are pleasures for evermore** (Psalm 16:11).

Learn to enjoy being with the Lord. You're His child, and you have a right to enjoy being with Him, because He wants that for you. This is part of your divine destiny in Jesus.

So, don't lose your joy. If you do, you won't find anything but trouble. The Devil will see to it.

James goes on to tell you another ingredient you need for your ministry.

Knowing this, that the trying of your faith worketh *patience.*

James 1:3

The trying of your faith worketh patience. Repeat that to yourself. "The trying of my faith worketh patience." God is saying that to you, so make up your mind right now that you won't depart from your faith. Stand on the Word of God in faith no matter what circumstance you face.

Suppose every time you asked God for something, you received it in three days. What would happen if one time God waited nine days to answer your prayer? You'd be a nervous wreck! But when you pray and then have to stand in faith as you wait for God's answer, it worketh patience in you.

"But, Brother Norvel," you say, "what good does it do me to have patience?"

I wish I had three or four books in which I could tell you fully. But since I don't, I'll give it all to you in one verse:

But let patience have her perfect work, that ye may be perfect and entire, wanting nothing.

James 1:4

Glory to God! Help me, Jesus, to have patience! Did you know this verse was in the Bible? Look at the last two words: "wanting nothing." If you ever really begin to walk in faith and patience, and refuse to lose your joy, you will end up wanting nothing. You will have everything! When you let patience have her perfect work God will work in you.

Now, James gives us a warning:

> **If any of you lack wisdom, let him ask of God, that giveth to all men liberally, and upbraideth not; and it shall be given him. But let him ask in faith, nothing wavering. For he that wavereth is like a wave of the sea driven with the wind and tossed. For let not that man think that he shall receive any thing of the Lord. A double minded man is unstable in all his ways.**
>
> **James 1:5-8**

In this passage James gives us two important ingredients we all need to fulfill our destinies in God: wisdom and faith. We must dig for these spiritual treasures. We must actively reach out and take them.

Verse 8 says, **A double minded man is unstable in all his ways.** But I guarantee you this: If you have faith, patience and joy, you will not be double-minded. You become double-minded when you don't believe the truth of God's Word. And the Devil is always there to convince you to believe something else.

So don't let the Devil persuade you to believe something other than God's truth. Believe for total victory in Jesus' name. Until you see the manifestation, stay in faith. Establish your faith in the Lord Jesus Christ.

Resist the Devil

Another ministry principle James gives us is this: devil resistance.

> **Submit yourselves therefore to God. *Resist the devil*, and he will flee from you.**
>
> **James 4:7**

I'm going to deal with this more in another chapter, but I want to touch on it here. When you start drawing close to Jesus with an open heart in the search for truth, you'd better be ready to resist the Devil.

When that young woman I told you about earlier was working hard in high school and college to get straight A's (her name is even in *Who's Who Among Students in American Universities and Colleges!*), she probably didn't know what God would be doing with her once she graduated. She probably had no idea that one day she would be casting out devils.

"Casting out devils?" you ask. "Oh, Brother Norvel, I couldn't do that! Not me. I'll save that for my husband. I'll go get my pastor."

Are you kidding? *You* can resist the Devil. A devil will obey you if you command it to go in Jesus' name. Just tell it, "You foul devil, in Jesus' name, turn this person loose and *go right now! Go!*" You do that in faith and that devil will start whimpering and run off.

Devils don't go anywhere unless you show them you know what you're talking about.

So many full-gospel churches in America are messed up in their beliefs. The Bible teaches that devils cause diseases, not God, as so many teach. You can't show me anywhere in the New Testament where God ever put diseases upon His children or other people.

"Well," somebody might say, "this disease might not be caused by a devil." That's like saying honey might not be sweet! But honey *is* sweet. You have to watch yourself to keep from making foolish statements like that.

Now, you do live in the natural realm where you can do stupid things and get sick. For instance, you could wallow around for an hour in the snow with a sleeveless shirt on and catch a cold. But I'm talking about diseases that attach themselves to your body to kill you. Those diseases are caused by a devil!

You have to *command* devils to leave. You can't be nice about it. If a person has a backache or a bad cold, you are supposed to lay your hands on him and pray in Jesus' name. But when you encounter a devil trying to kill somebody, and the spirit of death is already gripping that person, you have to say, "In Jesus' name, *go!* I break your power, you devil!"

The church belongs to Jesus. That means you will need to give up your own self-made doctrines if you're ever going to fulfill your destiny in Him. James 4:7 says that *you* are to resist the Devil. If you don't, he'll just be free to do his work.

Jesus said, **In my name shall they cast out devils** (Mark 16:17). *You* need to break the power of that devil and make it leave.

Many denominations and Spirit-filled, full-gospel Christians would say that a Christian can't have a devil. But Christians are sometimes too quick to make statements like that with no biblical foundation. I've cast devils out of Spirit-filled, tongue-talking Christians, so I know what I'm talking about when I say, whether they want them or not, a Christian can have a devil.

I meet many deaf believers who have been Pentecostal for years. They love God — and they are deaf. One night the Lord told me, "Cast that deaf spirit out of the deaf people sitting here in this service."

"But, Jesus," I said, "they're Pentecostal, and they've been coming to this church for twenty-five years. They are clean-living and Spirit-filled. They couldn't have a devil!"

But Jesus replied, "I said, cast that deaf spirit out of them! Just use My name and say, 'You deaf devil, *come out of them!*'" And when I have done that, I've seen Spirit-filled Christians fall flat on the floor and lie there shaking with their mouths open. I've seen them cry with loud voices like in Mark 1 *(see* verses 23-26), before both ears popped open and normal hearing returned!

Of course normal hearing came back. The deaf spirit was gone!

Jesus doesn't make Spirit-filled Christians deaf. And there are only two spiritual forces in the world: Jesus and the Devil. One of them does good, and one of them does damage. You have to make up your mind what you're going to believe.

Do you want your ministry to come forth? Then make up your mind now to be a Bible-believer, not a man-pleaser. It doesn't make any difference what everybody else believes. You are obligated to believe the Bible, not what another person, the entire town, denomination or even the whole world believes. It's what *you* believe that counts. So do you believe what the Lord said about casting out devils or don't you?

Be Willing To Demonstrate
Your Authority as a Believer

Rev. Kenneth E. Hagin said that Jesus once appeared to him while he was laying hands on people for healing in a church prayer line. Brother Hagin said that as he prayed for a woman dying of cancer, he looked around and saw Jesus standing nearby, watching him.

"You didn't pray for that woman right," Jesus said to Brother Hagin. "Break the power of that devil and make it leave her."

Suddenly, Brother Hagin saw a little monkey-like creature hanging on the woman's shoulder and around her neck. Then Jesus told him, "Command that thing to loose her and let her go free. Command it to get off these premises. This is My church, and it has My name. Devils have no right in My church."

So Brother Hagin told that demon, "In Jesus' name, you have to turn her loose now and let her go! Get off her!"

The creature replied, "I don't want to."

So Hagin said it again. "Get off her in Jesus' name!" And the creature dropped to the floor and whimpered. It was going to hang around her feet and climb back up on her until Brother Hagin said, "And get off these premises too!" "Well," the creature replied, "if you tell me to, I'm going to have to. But I don't want to. But if you tell me to in that name, I'm going to have to. But I don't want to."

"Oh, shut up and get out of here!" Brother Hagin said. And the monkey-like creature ran down the church aisle and out the door.

You don't hear too much about that kind of thing in Sunday school. But the result was that the poor sister dying with cancer was healed standing right there. Doctors had given her no hope. The devil left, and the Spirit of God came upon her and gave her a total healing.

You have to make the Devil leave. He's out to steal your ministry and your destiny, and he isn't going to leave you unless you *make* him. As a servant of God, you have the freedom to use Jesus' name, so use it to make the Devil leave. You have a right to do that. In fact, you will *have* to do it if you want your ministry to come forth in its fullness!

Now let's move on to Chapter 3 to establish the importance of grounding yourself in sound Bible doctrine as you seek Jesus in your destiny search.

—3—

Doctrines and Gifts

If you are ever going to reach your divine destiny that God is calling you to, you are going to have to become grounded in God's Word. You're going to have to know the Bible.

Preach the word; be instant in season, out of season; reprove, rebuke, exhort with all longsuffering and doctrine. For the time will come when they will not endure sound doctrine; but after their own lusts shall they heap to themselves teachers, having itching ears; and they shall turn away their ears from the truth, and shall be turned unto fables.

2 Timothy 4:2-4

Paul's words to Timothy, in this passage tell us how important it is to hold to sound doctrine.

In Jesus' day, the Sadducees had developed a doctrine that denied the resurrection. And they tried to trick Jesus with a religious question based on that doctrine in Matthew 22:23-28. Now look at Jesus' reply.

Jesus answered and said unto them, Ye do err, *not knowing the scriptures,* nor the power of God.

Matthew 22:29

The Lord Jesus said the Sadducees' doctrine was wrong because it wasn't based on the Scriptures. He said they

51

didn't know the Scriptures. And that is where people miss it most.

Where you and I make most of our mistakes is in not knowing the Scriptures. Once you learn this, your whole life will change.

God has only blessings for you and your family. And if you know the Scriptures and obey God, they will come upon you.

If you're not experiencing God's blessings, my brother, then you probably **do err, not knowing the scriptures, nor the power of God.** Because if your doctrine — your believing — is wrong, you won't experience them.

If you want to know the truth about the matter, many churches will never experience God's blessings until they change their doctrine. It doesn't matter if those churches exist for another five hundred years. God will never bless them, because their doctrine is not His.

Jesus used the Scriptures to show the Sadducees where their believing was wrong.

> **As touching the resurrection of the dead, have ye not read that which was spoken unto you by God, saying, I am the God of Abraham, and the God of Isaac, and the God of Jacob? God is not the God of the dead, but of the living.**
>
> **Matthew 22:31,32**

Now look at how the people listening reacted to Jesus' words.

> **When the multitude heard this, they were astonished at his doctrine.**
>
> **Matthew 22:33**

I don't doubt that. People are still astonished at Jesus' doctrine.

So, to find and walk in God's destiny for your life, my brother, you will have to establish your beliefs on the truth of God's Word. Then, after you do that, you're going to have to make up your mind, my sister, to never change. Always keep your doctrine straight. I don't care if you end up speaking to fifty thousand people and your ministry is worth one hundred million dollars — don't ever change!

The Doctrine of Baptisms

The Bible gives us the basic doctrines you should concentrate on as you get established in the truth.

I want to highlight a few of these doctrines. First, let's look at the doctrine of *baptisms.* Notice that the Bible says baptisms, plural.

Therefore leaving the principles of the doctrine of Christ, let us go on unto perfection; not laying again the foundation of repentance from dead works, and of faith toward God, of the doctrine of baptisms, and of laying on of hands, and of resurrection of the dead, and of eternal judgment.

Hebrews 6:1,2

Now I know of a certain denomination that teaches there is only one baptism — baptism in water. But, the Bible says there are many baptisms. This is a basic doctrine of the church.

When you are born again by the Spirit of God, you are baptized into the body of Christ. Then after you are born again, you need to be baptized in water. And either before or after your water baptism, you should be baptized in the Holy Spirit to receive power from on high. You may even be baptized in the Holy Spirit at the same time you are born again. So there is salvation baptism, water baptism and Holy Spirit baptism.

The Doctrine of the Laying On of Hands
...and of laying on of hands....

Besides the doctrine of baptisms, you have to understand the doctrine of the laying on of hands. Then you need to make your hands available to God, glory to God. You should make all parts of your body available to God because your body is a temple of the Holy Ghost. (Romans 6:19; 1 Corinthians 6:19,20.) God Himself lives within you in the Person of the Holy Spirit. But zero in on your hands. If you don't make your hands available to Him, you will never find the fullness of your destiny.

The laying on of hands is a doctrine of the church. So don't argue about it; only obey it.

You also have to give your mouth to God, because of all the members of your body, your mouth and your hands are the two most important. Jesus said if you are willing to go out and open your mouth for God, He would open His mouth for you.

Whosoever shall confess me before men, him shall the Son of man also confess before the angels of God: But he that denieth me before men shall be denied before the angels of God.

Luke 12:8,9

Jesus also said that if you are questioned by church or civil authorities about your testimony for Him, the Holy Spirit will give you the words to speak.

When they bring you unto the synagogues, and unto magistrates, and powers, take ye no thought how or what thing ye shall answer, or what ye shall say: For the Holy Ghost shall teach you in the same hour what ye ought to say.

Luke 12:11,12

When I was saved, it took me a while to figure out that I needed to make my mouth and hands available to God. Before I gave my life to Jesus, I just went to church to be nice. But after I was born again, I *wanted* to go to church. That was definitely better than just going to be nice. But it was a far cry from finding my ministry and destiny in God.

You see, I still hadn't given my mouth to God. After I became willing to do that, I began to witness to people about Jesus. Then I found out I was ignorant. (When you're a business executive, it amazes you to learn that you are ignorant!) When I came face to face with a dying person, I discovered I didn't know what to do. The person would tell me, "I'm dying with this disease. I'm supposed to be dead in three weeks. Can you help me, Mr. Hayes?"

I'd say, "Well, uh...."

"Mr. Hayes, you pray for people, don't you?"

"Uh, yes, I do," I'd reply. But what kind of prayer was I supposed to pray in a life-and-death situation? I didn't know back then that the power of God could flow through my words and hands to heal the sick and raise them off a deathbed.

Somebody would say, "Mr. Hayes, I have club feet. Can you help me?"

I'd say, "Well, uh, you see, uh, God can do anything."

What a lame answer that was! If you were God, and the only ministry you had operating around the world was a bunch of Christians saying, "God can do anything," you'd be in trouble. Even the Devil believes that.

Are you kidding? If you have enough sense to find a church, you ought to know that God can do anything. Look around at the world He spoke into existence — the lakes, the oceans, the mountains. You ought to know that a God Who can speak this world into existence can do anything He chooses to do. I could see that by the time I was three years old.

So just saying, "God can do anything" was no testimony at all to a man who was asking for new feet.

The man asked me, "Do you believe Jesus makes new feet?"

"Well, uh...."

"I never did see Him do that in any church I went to, Brother Norvel."

Remember this as long as you live: God isn't moved by church services. Church services are supposed to be moved by *Him.* God doesn't think according to how you think. He thinks according to His Word, and He never changes. He's the same all the time.

That man's feet weren't going to be healed because of some programmed church service that was based on man's opinions. But his feet *could* get healed through the laying on of hands, because that's Bible doctrine.

The Doctrine of Faith

Another Bible doctrine you need to keep straight is the doctrine of faith.

Let us go on unto perfection; not laying again the foundation ... of faith toward God....

Hebrews 6:1

Many of my friends in the ministry who travel around the country teaching faith have no earthly idea what it is.

You'd be surprised by the number of people today who teach faith because they heard and memorized Rev. Kenneth E. Hagin's tapes. Now, if a person memorizes Brother Hagin's tapes, I guarantee that person can teach faith. Brother Hagin is a faith man if I ever met one.

But just because you memorized somebody's tapes and teach faith yourself, that doesn't mean you know anything *about* faith. You could just be teaching what you memorized and are living in unbelief.

So when you come upon a situation that looks impossible, be careful not to say, "How could God fix anything like that?" Maybe you never saw that problem supernaturally dealt with in the church you were raised in. But, remember, that church may have been as sick as you were!

You have to watch yourself real closely. You can't judge God by a church service or by what you know. You have to judge Him according to the Bible.

Can blind people receive their sight from God today in our modern, jet-age church? Sure they can, as soon as they start crying out to Him in faith for their sight.

An example of faith at work is found in the story of Bartimaeus, the blind beggar who got healed beside the road.

They came to Jericho: and as he went out of Jericho with his disciples and a great number of people, blind Bartimaeus, the son of Timaeus sat by

the highway side begging. And when he heard that it was Jesus of Nazareth, he began to cry out, and say, Jesus, thou son of David, have mercy on me.

Mark 10:46,47

What did Bartimaeus do? He cried out, "Jesus, thou son of David, have mercy on me!" But a great many of the people walking with Jesus told Bartimaeus, "Shut up! Be quiet! Hold your peace!"

And many charged him that he should hold his peace: but he cried the more a great deal, Thou son of David, have mercy on me.

v. 48

But the more the people yelled at Bartimaeus, the more he cried out for Jesus. The Bible says he yelled "a great deal." That's the opposite of a little bit! And Jesus noticed that:

And Jesus stood still, and commanded him to be called. And they call the blind man, saying unto him, Be of good comfort, rise; he calleth thee. And he, casting away his garment, rose, and came to Jesus. And Jesus answered and said unto him, What wilt thou that I should do unto thee? The blind man said unto him, Lord, that I might receive my sight. And Jesus said unto him, Go thy way; *thy faith hath made thee whole.* And immediately he received his sight, and followed Jesus in the way.

Mark 10:49-52

When Jesus recognized Bartimaeus' faith, He said, thy faith hath made thee whole. Jesus said to me one day,

"When some of these blind people start believing that Scripture, they'll receive their sight."

Why?

Because heaven always picks up on faith. In fact, the only way heaven can come to earth to help meet people's needs is through faith. And faith is believing something that you don't yet see.

When was the last time Jesus was able to "pick up on" *your* faith?

"Well, Brother Norvel, I'm trying to believe the book of Hebrews. I've been listening to tapes...."

That will help you to some extent, but you'll have to get beyond the tapes, my brother. You'll have to get the book of Hebrews on the inside of you, my sister.

You need to understand that faith — *your* faith — is your answer. Your faith has nothing to do with me — nothing!

If I have faith in God or in a verse of Scripture, God will give me what I'm believing Him for. I don't have to have everybody in Houston, Texas, believing God for me!

If I have sense enough to believe the Bible for myself — even one verse of Scripture — I could read it and say, "Lord Jesus, I know You love me. I believe You died on the cross and shed Your blood for me. And I know I sure do love You, Jesus. I know that Your greatest desire is for me to show You that I trust You.

"So, Jesus, I'm going to show You that I trust You. I believe this verse of Scripture right here [whatever verse applies to my need]. My body needs to be healed, Jesus. So I stand on Your Word for my healing right now." "My child is lost; he's on drugs and living with somebody outside of marriage, Jesus. So I stand in the gap and intercede now, calling my child's name before You."

After you've done that, stick with what you believe. Don't quit.

Now faith is the substance of things hoped for, the evidence of things not seen.

Hebrews 11:1

According to this Scripture, faith is not seen, and faith is right now. So always remember: You can't make God answer your prayer in a week. But if your faith — your believing — stays in line with the Scriptures you found that deal with your situation, the manifestation of God's promise will always come at the right time. And if you have to wait for a while, you'll understand why.

Now, if you start wavering and doubting, you could bog down the manifestation of your answer for years, even though God may want to give it to you in a week. But if you keep believing, your faith will get stronger.

Maybe you've been lazy and nonchalant about your prayer life. Or maybe you haven't even taken time to develop a prayer life! Maybe you think you can contact heaven without one. If you do, I have news for you: You have a great shock coming! There is no way to contact heaven from this earth without prayer.

I'm telling you, you'd better develop some kind of prayer life if you want to live out the destiny God has planned for you. Pray while you're taking a shower. Pray as you walk the floor. Whatever it takes, develop a prayer life. Don't let yourself go for days, weeks or months without praying. It will get your thinking messed up! You'll start wondering if your own children love you. You'll whine and worry about all kinds of lies from the Devil.

But if you'll develop your prayer life, everything will become amazingly clear to you. Your destiny will become clearer every day. You'll be able to see into the heavens, because God unfolds His truth to His prayer warriors.

But first, you will have to get your doctrine straight about faith, so you know how to pray.

Don't Listen to the Devil

Of course, the Devil will try to push you off your stance of faith to make you miss your destiny in God completely. But you can decide not to listen to the Devil when he comes to you with his lies!

Let's take a look at 1 Timothy 4:1:

Now the Spirit speaketh expressly, that in the latter times some shall depart from the faith, giving heed to seducing spirits, and doctrines of devils.

Please don't let this verse that talks about listening to "seducing spirits and doctrines of devils" refer to you. A lot of Spirit-filled Christians open their mouths and say, "Well, you know, I've had this disease for a long time. It just might not be God's will to heal me. He might be getting glory out of my being sick." But that kind of thinking is nowhere in the Bible. These people don't know that they're listening to seducing spirits and doctrines of devils. They didn't get those thoughts from God the Father or Jesus or the Holy Spirit, and they certainly didn't get those ideas from the Bible. A devil put those thoughts into their minds.

Don't Depart From the Faith

First Timothy 4:1 says that **in the latter times some shall depart from the faith.** So don't be a part of that crowd and depart from the faith. Don't depart from believing that you receive the answer to your prayer before you see it or you'll miss your destiny.

Faith is not "seeing before believing." If you have to wait until you see something to believe it, you're not in faith. If God promised something to you in the Bible, stand boldly on that promise and claim it in Jesus' name. Talk like you have your answer. Act like you have it. Sing like you have it, especially when you don't see a thing. You'll find that if you do that, the storm you're facing will disappear. And Jesus Christ Himself will do for you what He did for that blind beggar beside the road. He will pick up on your faith because you didn't waver. You just kept on believing.

You have to become established in sound doctrine, my brother, before you'll ever find the destiny God has for you. You must have those doctrines in Hebrews 6:1 and 2 straight, from baptisms — to faith — to the laying on of hands.

So make your hands available to the Lord to find the fullness of your divine destiny. You may be able to fulfill a part of it even if you don't understand some of these doctrines. But you'll never be able to walk in the fullness of your destiny until you are strongly established in every one of them.

The Gifts of the Spirit

And while you're becoming established in the Bible's important doctrines, make sure you also study the gifts of the Holy Spirit listed in 1 Corinthians 12:4-11. You need these gifts. They are important "helpers" to your destiny and your ministry. The truth is, you can't do much for the Lord on this earth without the gifts of the Spirit. You will need all nine gifts of the Holy Spirit at one time or another in the ministry God has planned for you. But you have to develop a hunger for these gifts.

Now there are diversities of gifts, but the same Spirit. And there are differences of administrations, but the same Lord. And there are diversities of operations, but it is the same God which worketh all in all. But the manifestation of the Spirit is given to every man to profit withal. For to one is given by the Spirit the word of wisdom; to another the word of knowledge by the same Spirit; to another faith by the same Spirit; to another the gifts of healing by the same Spirit; to another the working of miracles; to another prophecy; to another discerning of spirits; to another divers kinds of tongues; to another the interpretation of tongues: But all these worketh that one and the selfsame Spirit, dividing to every man severally as he will.

1 Corinthians 12:4-11

The Gift of Faith

Sometimes you will need the gift of faith. This isn't the kind of faith you receive when you read the Bible and believe God's promises. It's the kind of faith that comes when God's power comes upon you and you say to a devil, "In Jesus' name, be quiet! Shut up! In Jesus' name, come out of him!" The gift of faith can drop on you so that you can even cast the devil out of somebody who is addicted to hard drugs — even heroin!

There have been times when the gift of faith dropped on me and I cast the devil out of people who were high on drugs so fast, that it made my head swim! The Holy Ghost knocked them out on the floor. They went down high on the needle and got up later totally sober. And they never took any more drugs!

All this happened because God's supernatural power came upon me to cause me to do something I couldn't have done in the natural. This is what the gift of faith does, through supernatural power and supernatural faith. As you walk in the ministry God has for you, this kind of spiritual gift will begin to manifest as the Spirit wills. (1 Cor. 12:11.)

The young woman I spoke about in Chapter 2 who chose to go a step further than the ordinary Christian saw these gifts of the Holy Spirit manifest through her. And when *you* honestly and sincerely choose to do the same thing — when you faithfully pray and read the Bible and refuse to allow men to give you their carnal opinions or doctrines — get ready. The Spirit of God will anoint you and give you His gifts! Not only that, but you will be amazed at how the Bible unfolds before you as the Holy Spirit teaches you by revelation.

Ministry Gifts

According to the dictionary, *doctrine* means, among other things, something that is taught.[1]

[1] *Webster's New World College Dictionary*, Third Edition (New York: Simon & Schuster, Inc., 1996), "doctrine." p.402.

Paul tells us in Ephesians 4 that Jesus puts certain people in particular positions in the church for the purpose of "growing up" the body of Christ.

And he gave some, apostles; and some, prophets; and some, evangelists; and some, pastors and teachers; for the perfecting of the saints, for the work of the ministry, for the edifying of the body of Christ: Till we all come in the unity of the faith, and of the knowledge of the Son of God, unto a perfect [mature] man, unto the measure of the stature of the fulness of Christ.

Ephesians 4:11-13

Apostle, prophet, evangelist, pastor and teacher are all positions in the church. Let's look at two of these positions: evangelist and apostle.

First, let's consider the office of evangelist. The title of evangelist goes with a particular calling of God.

Rev. Kenneth E. Hagin said Jesus once explained the office of New Testament evangelist to him. People can run newspaper ads advertising meetings at which "evangelist so-and-so" will speak. But evangelist so-and-so may just *think* he's an evangelist. Brother Hagin said Jesus told him that a New Testament evangelist must have the gifts of healing and the gift of working of miracles operating all the time in his or her ministry. Without those, a person is not a true evangelist, even though God may have called them into a pulpit ministry.

Jesus also told Brother Hagin that many people who call themselves evangelists actually are exhorters. Then he gave Brother Hagin several modern examples of the true New Testament evangelist.

The first example Jesus gave Brother Hagin was Oral Roberts. Brother Roberts has the gifts of healing operating through his hands and the gift of working of miracles manifest in his ministry. He is an authentic New Testament evangelist, set in that office by God.

Jesus' second example of a New Testament evangelist was T. L. Osborn. Brother Osborn is both an evangelist and an apostle. The gifts of healing and of working of miracles manifest through him. He ministers to multitudes who don't know anything about God. And God has sent him to foreign lands to raise up churches.

I know Brother Osborn well enough to know that he always is happiest on the mission field. He isn't satisfied to just speak in churches in the United States. I remember one meeting where he and I were both speaking. The Spirit of God moved strongly as he spoke. And when he gave an altar call, five or six hundred people must have responded.

Afterward, when we met, he shook his head. "Norvel," he said, "it's wonderful to see the Lord work. Meetings like this are fine for other people. But my heart is on the mission field."

Brother Osborn told me his heart yearned to look out over the hills and see countless multitudes of people. Many cripples came to his meetings. Some traveled for two days to get there. He said he longed to see the power of God come from heaven and blanket the whole hillside.

How To Know God's Call to a Ministry Office

An old preacher once told me how he answered people who asked him how they could know if God had called them to preach. "I always suggest to people," he said, "don't preach unless you have to. If you have to preach, then you know you are called. If you don't have to preach, you'll always wonder if God called you."

In other words, that man was saying if there is a drive inside of you to preach, then God has called you. If you want to preach so much that you can't sleep at night and you have to go out and preach to the trees, that's when you know you are called. I'm not sure I totally agree with him, but it's pretty good advice. A lot of people aren't called to preach. They just learn how to preach.

What I do know to be completely true is, if you want to search out God's destiny for your life, you need to have your beliefs firmly grounded on the Word of God. Learn the basic doctrines of the church — the ones the Bible says are important — then stick with them. Don't ever change. If you keep your doctrine straight, the Devil will have a hard time stealing your destiny call.

The Devil wants to corrupt everything within you in his attempts at stealing your destiny in Christ. This is our next subject in Chapter 4.

—4—

Don't Let the Devil Steal Your God-Given Talents

L*et me tell you a little more about the Devil now.*

God once made a creature to be His right-hand man. He gave him exceptional looks, intelligence, wisdom, power and great musical ability. The Devil was that creature. God allowed him to go up into His holy mountain and walk up and down in the stones of fire.

But after a time this creature began to take stock of what he had and wondered how great he could become. He began to get prideful. And he tried to conquer God.

For thou hast said in thine heart, I will ascend into heaven, I will exalt my throne above the stars of God: I will sit also upon the mount of the congregation, in the sides of the north.

Isaiah 14:13

Even if you're the prettiest woman in the world, or the most handsome man, you'd better not think you are. If you do, you'll get into pride. Serve Jesus. Worship the God Who made you. You can stay good-looking all of your life. The glory of Almighty God will come upon you.

God makes every human being unique. He personally made you and gave you certain abilities and talents. Nobody else in the world is exactly like you. So don't ever say to God, "I wish I looked like somebody else," or, "I wish I could do this." No. Be satisfied with who God made you. He made you exactly the way He wants you to be.

Jesus Knows What He Has Put in You

You are going to have to give up your talents completely to the Lord as you obey God to fulfill your destiny.

Different people have to give up different things to serve the Lord. Jesus spoke in a vision to one man I know of when He called him into a traveling ministry and asked him to pray for the sick. This man was serving as a pastor and didn't want a traveling ministry. He wanted to stay home with his wife and children and take care of his congregation. He told the Lord all he wanted was a small church.

That didn't set well with Jesus. With fire in His eyes, the Lord told the minister, "You don't know what you can do for Me, but I do. I know what I can make out of you. Now obey Me. Who called you into the ministry?"

"You did, Lord," the man replied.

"Well, then," Jesus said, "obey Me."

"Yes Sir, Lord," the minister answered.

That was many years ago. And that minister, who was content to pastor a little, small-town Pentecostal church, ended up founding a Bible school that has touched countless thousands of lives with God's power.

That's right, I'm talking about Rev. Kenneth E. Hagin again. I've ministered with him over the years, and he doesn't ever change. He's just as precious and sweet a man today as he was when he drove around the country preaching in churches. He carried his books in his car trunk and his wife, Oretha, sold them at the meetings.

Brother Hagin teaches the same things now that he taught when he started out. Graduates of Rhema Bible Training Center in Broken Arrow, Oklahoma, have a work on every continent of the world. Glory be to Jesus forevermore!

I know of another man who paid a great price to do what the Lord called him to.

Years ago, I was speaking in a big crusade-type meeting and this minister and his wife were sitting on the front row. After the service, he came to my room and introduced himself. He said that another minister had told him about me but that we had never met before. Then he said, "You read my mail in your message today."

I'd spoken that day about what happens when one marriage partner rebels against God's call on his or her mate. That's what happened to me when God called me, and that's what had happened to him.

Listen to me: If you are married and God calls your spouse to serve Him, don't rebel against that call! If you do, you will miss the call of God on your life as well.

This particular man and his first wife had a good ministry going on their own. Then the Lord called him to go and help with the ministry of one of his relatives.

But his wife refused to go with him. She believed she had her own ministry, and ended up leaving her husband to pursue it. Finally, they divorced.

But God was at work in that man's life as his ministry broadened into teaching, preaching and healing, with great results. He didn't intend to remarry. But after some time he met the right woman. They married, and he and his new wife began ministering together, clearly with God's blessing.

That man's first wife could have been the one ministering with him. But it was too late. She hadn't been willing, so God couldn't work through her. The Devil will lie to anybody who will listen, whether you are in the ministry or not.

You have to be willing, my friend, to obey God. Don't ever swallow the Devil's lies.

You might ask how a second marriage could be of the Lord when the first one was of the Lord. Well, God brings many people together. But if they don't walk with God, they can move completely out of His will.

A Christian can marry another Christian and eventually have the marriage fall apart. That person might say, "I guess it just wasn't God's will that we marry." Well, that might be true, but not necessarily. One partner, or both, could have moved totally out of God's will.

Walking with God involves day-to-day decisions. God knows what He can make out of you. When God called me, I didn't know what talents He had placed in me. And you probably don't know much about your talents, either. Just don't let the Devil or the people he sends your way mess you up. Let God mold you. God is the only One Who can do it. You're ten times the person in His eyes than you are in your own eyes. He sees who you can be and what you can do for Him.

Let God Decide What Talents
You Have and How To Use Them

The Devil would like to convince you that your God-ordained talents aren't anything special.

I really enjoyed working with Kathryn Kuhlman. I once heard her say that she had no talent or ability of her own whatsoever, as far as she knew. She was born in Concordia, Missouri. And when she was just a little bitty, teeny girl raised as a Methodist, God called her into the ministry. It happened one day as she sat in the balcony of her church.

In those days, women preachers weren't very popular. (In the denomination I came out of they *still* aren't popular.) God called Kathryn Kuhlman into a traveling ministry, and as a teenager, she preached in cities of all sizes.

But church people hated her because she was a young woman preacher and wouldn't put her up in motels or let her stay in their homes. So when she started out, she had to sleep in chicken coops.

I eventually came to know Sister Kuhlman personally. I carried a special pass that she gave me so I could get into her meetings. Thousands of people would wait outside trying to get in. Sometimes no building in America was big enough to hold the crowd.

Why?

Because God touched her and molded her into the person she was born to be.

Sister Kuhlman had more of God's power in her ministry than any ten men I've ever seen. (And I've been around just about all of them in America.) I don't know of ten preachers living right now who have as much power as she did.

And Rev. Kuhlman paid a price to have that kind of power flowing through her. She once told me that it was lonely to have that power. She said she was full of joy, peace and contentment in her spirit, but her natural life was lonely.

"Thank God I have Him," she said. "It's worth every minute of natural loneliness to see the Holy Spirit work. But I must stay alone with God to have this power. After a meeting, I must go straight to my room and shut the door. Sometimes I can go eat a meal with people and that type of thing. But I can't rub shoulders with the world and have this kind of power from God."

So whatever it takes for you, don't let the Devil steal your God-given talents. Remember where your priorities should be. When you learn of the great miracles God worked through Sister Kuhlman and of the huge crowds that followed her, you might be tempted to say, "I want Kathryn Kuhlman's ministry." But if you want what's best for you, you won't want someone else's ministry. You'll want the ministry that God has for you.

Seek God's Destiny for *You*

I don't want Kathryn Kuhlman's ministry.

Why?

Because I'm not Kathryn Kuhlman.

I want God's ministry for Norvel Hayes. I want to do what He wants *me* to do. All I'm interested in is obeying God. I don't want to dream up my own ministry or my own way of doing things. There are too many of man's ways in the church today already. You've got to be kidding. Who would want to go their own way when they can go God's way? Learn to be led.

For as many as are led by the Spirit of God, they are the sons of God.

Romans 8:14

If you are led by the Spirit of God, then you are a son of God. And the Spirit of God will lead you in the way that's best for you. God's plan for your life is the best one for you. He wants to make *you* who He intended *you* to be.

Remember, God created Lucifer for a specific purpose. But Lucifer wanted to go a different way. Ezekiel says:

Thou hast been in Eden the garden of God; every precious stone was thy covering, the sardius, topaz, and the diamond, the beryl, the onyx, and the jasper, the sapphire, the emerald, and the carbuncle, and gold: the workmanship of thy tabrets and of thy pipes was prepared in thee in the day that thou wast created.

Ezekiel 28:13

When God creates you, He puts things in you for a special time, and for His glory. In Esther 4:14, Mordecai reminded Queen Esther of her destiny and its appointed times:

For if thou altogether holdest thy peace at this time, then shall there enlargement and deliverance arise to the Jews from another place; but thou and thy father's house shall be destroyed: and who knoweth whether thou art come to the kingdom for such a time as this?

When I was younger, I didn't use what God prepared in me for His glory. No one trained me as a kid the way

I was supposed to be trained. But thank God for Jesus and the Holy Spirit!

As I grew in my walk with the Lord, it became important for me to spend time with the right people. I looked for some full-gospel folks who could help me enter into God's presence so He could mold me. God ordered my steps to move me to Cleveland, Tennessee, where I now live and where my ministry is based. I anticipate that what God brought me there for will happen at any time. And God has a destiny for you. Don't let the Devil tell you, "It's too late for you!" **For the gifts and calling of God are without repentance** (Romans 11:29).

When I was praying one day, the word of the Lord came unto me. He told me He brought me to Cleveland, Tennessee, to bring His power to that city.

"God," I said, "there are Pentecostal churches all over town. Those people know You better than I do."

But He wouldn't change.

So it wouldn't surprise me if at any time a great revival would break out like that town has never known, and last for months.

One February night, during a meeting I was holding in our Bible College auditorium, the Spirit of God came on me especially strong. There was a woman there who couldn't even stand up, much less walk, because of bone marrow cancer. You know what the Holy Ghost did for her? Glory to God. When God's power got through with her, she walked up and down the aisles!

When the Holy Spirit comes to do away with the works of hell, you can forget about what the Devil has tried to do to you. God can set you totally free! So don't let the Devil steal your talents or your destiny. It amazes me that most people live and die and never know who God wants them to be.

Now let's get back to that "beautiful Devil." Good looks can be a blessing or a curse. They have messed up some people, though I've never really had any great problem with that.

God gives some people great talents at birth. He gives them "tabrets and pipes" — talents and abilities — exactly as He chooses. But sometimes when these people become teenagers or adults, they sell their talents to the Devil.

Let's look at Ezekiel 28 again.

> **Thou art the anointed cherub that covereth; and I have set thee so: thou wast upon the holy mountain of God; thou hast walked up and down in the midst of the stones of fire.**
>
> **Ezekiel 28:14**

My God in Heaven. God gave Lucifer great talent when He first created him. He gave him great power and privileges and a special mission.

Why didn't God make him perfect so he wouldn't rebel? Now you need to notice this. He *did* make him perfect.

> **Thou wast perfect in thy ways from the day that thou wast created, till iniquity was found in thee.**
>
> **v. 15**

So you'd better watch those blessings God gave you. Appreciate them every day. Use that talent God gave you for Him. I understand that we all need a job to make a living. But make sure that you take time to use your talents and abilities for God. If you don't, I warn you that they can become a curse to you. Don't let Satan redirect your blessings and talents like he misdirected the talents and blessings God gave to him.

By the multitude of thy merchandise they have filled the midst of thee with violence, and thou hast sinned: therefore I will cast thee as profane out of the mountain of God: and I will destroy thee, O covering cherub, from the midst of the stones of fire.

Ezekiel 28:16

Sin separates a man or woman from God. And when you're separated from God, you're on the way to destruction. So make sure that you stay in contact with God Almighty, my brother. Make sure that God can talk to you on the inside, my sister. God lives in your belly, not your head.

Don't Trade the Anointing

And make sure you do what God anointed you to do. Your anointing will be different from anyone else's, because God's creations are unique.

The anointing is more precious than gold or silver. I wouldn't trade God's anointing on my life for a town full of million-dollar bills. I wouldn't sell the anointing on me for the world and everything in it. It's not for sale. More than anything else, I'd rather have a direct line to God so He can talk to me and I can worship and praise Him. I want God to be able to talk to me when He wants me to do something for Him.

Start thanking God for the anointing on your life, remembering to let Him put on you whatever anointing He wants to. He placed a strong anointing on Lucifer. He appointed him to a high position, putting him in charge of angels.

God let Lucifer go up into His own holy mountain and walk up and down amid the stones of fire. He let him into his precious garden and endowed him with all kinds of riches and wealth.

And God gave him great looks. That is what destroyed him.

Thine heart was lifted up because of thy beauty, thou hast corrupted thy wisdom by reason of thy brightness: I will cast thee to the ground, I will lay thee before kings, that they may behold thee. Thou hast defiled thy sanctuaries by the multitude of thine iniquities, by the iniquity of thy traffick; therefore will I bring forth a fire from the midst of thee, it shall devour thee, and I will bring thee to ashes upon the earth in the sight of all them that behold thee.

Ezekiel 28:17,18

Satan's great beauty shouldn't have brought his downfall. If God made him beautiful, it must have been a good thing. Why can't you be a beautiful person without backsliding?

Great Looks and a Great Mind

If God has given you great looks, use them for your spouse and your looks will grow sweeter all the time. They will be a blessing, not a curse. Don't dress so others will notice you. Dress for your spouse.

You may have a million-dollar-making mind. If you do, use it for God, or it can become a curse for you.

At one time Lucifer was good-looking and had great wisdom. But because he began to think about how

79

beautiful he was, his heart became lifted up and his wisdom was corrupted. Now he has no more wisdom.

Wisdom is one of the greatest gifts God ever imparted to a human being. And He gives it to men generously. Remember, James wrote, **If any of you lack wisdom, let him ask of God, that giveth to all men liberally, and upbraideth not; and it shall be given him** (James 1:5). In fact, if I could ask God for only one gift, it would be His wisdom.

If you don't watch it, the Devil will take any good thing that God has given to you and use it to destroy you. So whatever "pipes, tabrets, merchandise" or other good things God has put in you, use them for Him.

The Devil started out that way as Lucifer, the shining one, but he changed and lost everything. He lost his beauty, authority, wisdom and even his mind.

God gave us a mind and some special things to do with it. One of those special things God wants us to use our minds for is to speak things into existence. Abraham's life is a good example of this.

Cometh this blessedness then upon the circumcision only, or upon the uncircumcision also? for we say that faith was reckoned to Abraham for righteousness.

How was it then reckoned? when he was in circumcision, or in uncircumcision? Not in circumcision, but in uncircumcision.

And he received the sign of circumcision, a seal of the righteousness of the faith which he had yet being uncircumcised: that he might be the father of all them that believe, though they be

not circumcised; that righteousness might be imputed unto them also:

And the father of circumcision to them who are not of the circumcision only, but who also walk in the steps of that faith of our father Abraham, which he had being yet uncircumcised.

For the promise, that he should be the heir of the world, was not to Abraham, or to his seed, through the law, but through the righteousness of faith.

For if they which are of the law be heirs, faith is made void, and the promise made of none effect:

Because the law worketh wrath: for where no law is, there is no transgression.

Therefore it is of faith, that it might be by grace; to the end the promise might be sure to all the seed; not to that only which is of the law, but to that also which is of the faith of Abraham; who is the father of us all,

(As it is written, I have made thee a father of many nations,) before him whom he [Abraham] believed, even God, who quickeneth the dead, and calleth those things which be not as though they were.

Who against hope believed in hope, that he might become the father of many nations, according to that which was spoken, So shall thy seed be.

And being not weak in faith, he considered not his own body now dead, when he was about an hundred years old, neither yet the deadness of Sarah's womb:

> He staggered not at the promise of God
> through unbelief; but was strong in faith, giving
> glory to God.
>
> **Romans 4:9-20**

If you're in right-standing with God and know what you need to know about Him, and your relationship with Him, you can speak things into existence.

A modern example of this is T. L. Osborn. Brother Osborn is, as far as I know, one of the greatest missionaries since the days of Paul. He did his preaching outdoors. I can't really say enough about him. He didn't say, "How many people do we have tonight?" He said, "How many acres of human beings do we have tonight?"

Now, it is said that Brother Osborn has preached to more live human beings than anybody in history, including Paul. For over thirty years, Rev. Osborn preached — some nights till 2 or 3 a.m. — to 400,000 people at one time. They used to measure his crowds by the acre.

His meetings were so large that it was impossible for him to lay hands on all those needing healing. When you're preaching to 200,000 people, you can't have a healing line. So he would pray that God's healing power would cover the hillside — and cripples would begin to walk.

You may have great abilities. Fine. Use them for God.

"But the world wants them," you say.

Satan is the god of this world. (2 Corinthians 4:4.) The Devil wants everything you have because he lost out. But just because the Devil lost out doesn't mean that you have to lose out.

It's getting tougher all the time to live a Christian life and stay close to God if you don't worship Him or do very much for Him. Your mind winds up in the world of wondering.

"I wonder why my life is so sad?" you might ask. "I don't feel like I'm loved. I don't know what the Lord is doing with me, Brother Norvel."

"Well," I say, "I don't know what He's doing with you, that's for sure. Just worship God and praise Him. Give yourself totally to Him and He will show you what to do."

If God sees you worshiping Him and thanking Him for help, then I have news for you: help is on the way. But if you rebel against God and don't worship Him, you'll be wondering about Him the next time I see you.

Bow down before Him. Let Him work for you. God plainly told me, a church that worships Him together never splits. Fusses, fights and hard feelings are caused by the prideful minds of men. "I want a position," they say. "I don't like my pastor. I think I'll start a church myself. I think these people will follow me more than the pastor," and so on.

When God gave us a mind, He meant it for good. So don't let Satan's thoughts turn what was meant for good into evil. **Pride goeth before destruction, and an haughty spirit before a fall** (Proverbs 16:18).

Real Help

I know a pastor who has about twelve thousand people in his church. I asked him once if there were many people seeking publicity in such a large congregation.

"Oh my God," he replied. "All the time. Norvel, many famous people come floating into my church. They tell me, 'Reverend, I went to a certain voice school and I've been singing on national television for years. I've been doing this, and I've been doing that. So I'm available to sing special music at the church whenever you need me.'"

This pastor just tells them, "I appreciate your wanting to give yourself to the Lord. But I never let anybody take part in the church service until they prove themselves, first to God, and then to me."

In that church, people who sit in the back row every week are not asked to sing special music. But if they sit in the front row at every service they are able to attend, bring their Bible and are faithful for twelve months, that pastor might just let them sing a solo in his church.

If your pastor ever asks you to do anything for God and his church, count it as one of the greatest honors ever bestowed upon you. It doesn't matter whether you're sweeping the floor or teaching a Sunday school class. Take it as a great opportunity from God. Do it the best you can with all of your might because Paul said, **Whatsoever ye do, do it heartily, as to the Lord, and not unto men; knowing that of the Lord ye shall receive the reward of the inheritance: for ye serve the Lord Christ** (Colossians 3:23,24).

And keep a humble heart. Don't judge your pastor! I know you've heard this saying before, but it's the truth. I **had rather be a doorkeeper in the house of my God, than to dwell in the tents of wickedness** (Psalm 84:10). In other words, I would rather greet people at the church door on Sunday morning and be anointed, than be a rich pew sitter with no anointing because I hadn't done God's will.

Don't ever be like Lucifer and think that you're the greatest. Watch out for pride. That's one of the worst destiny traps in Satan's bag of tricks. You're just like I am, and if not for the Lord Jesus Christ, we wouldn't be worth fifteen cents. You weren't worth anything before you found Jesus, and you wouldn't be worth anything without Him. If God took His hand off of you, you'd be just like the Devil: out in the wasteland. Like Satan, you'd be a terror. But you and God will stay together as long as you stay humble, and always worship Him.

The Ultimate Terrorist

All they that know thee among the people shall be astonished at thee: thou shalt be a terror, and never shalt thou be any more.

Ezekiel 28:19

You will never find God's destiny for your life until you give yourself to God and resist the Devil, because Satan is the father of all terrorists. So, bind up devils and resist them in Jesus' name. James wrote:

Submit yourselves therefore to God. Resist the devil, and he will flee from you.

James 4:7

If you want to know how to keep the Devil off your back, join a church that knows and teaches how to keep him off your back. Learn God's ways. Don't lean on your own understanding. Listen to sermons and praise God. Sing to heaven. Be in church every time the doors are open. Sometimes I wonder if I go to church more than anybody else in America.

The Devil Blew It and He Wants You To Blow It

Can you imagine being buddy-buddy with God Almighty — working shoulder-to-shoulder with special permission from Him for many things — and losing all of that? That's what happened to the Devil, and he's angry.

If you're born again, you're going to heaven. And that's why the Devil is angry at you. He hates your guts!

Why?

Because he knows he will never be in heaven again.

The Devil knows heaven is glorious and beautiful, full of mansions and holy angels. He knows God's throne is there. And he doesn't want you there.

The Devil hates God because God caught him in his lying, thieving tricks. Have you ever noticed if you ever caught a person doing wrong, how he or she turned against you? If you are an employer, you've probably seen that.

The Scriptures clearly explain who the Devil is and why God had to deal with him the way He did. So, about all those things that bother you and buffet you, just know this: It is the Devil who will try to rob you of God's divine destiny for you. The Devil blew it and he wants you to blow it. As Lucifer he had God-given talents. But he lost them, and he wants to steal your God-given talents. God's Word tells us how far Lucifer fell because of his sin. Sin will separate you from your talents and the anointing, too. The Devil didn't resist sin, and he lost everything. But you have the authority to resist any wrong, and to resist the Devil.

Always remember this, believer in God: The Devil can't steal from you unless you let him. If you have been blessed with a million-dollar-making mind or you're not really sure right now what your talents are: Never forget — Satan wants to steal them. So God has given you the name of Jesus and the blood of Jesus as your defense. Walk in love and humble faith. Watch out for pride, and God will lead you every day to avoid the Devil's snares.

Now I'm going to show you how to exercise authority over the Devil in Chapter 5.

—5—

One Word: Resist

I hope by now you've been getting the point that if you're ever going to walk in the fulness of God's destiny for your life, you're going to have to learn to exercise authority over the Devil.

Dealing with the Devil is simple. You only need to do one thing — not the dozens of things you may have heard others teach. I can tell you in one word: The word is *resist.* But *you* have to do it. No one else can do it for you.

You must *resist.* That's all there is to it. There isn't anything else to it. You must resist the Devil and his works in Jesus' name.

How?

Use the name of Jesus against him.

The works of hell are anything bad that comes to your life. If you're sick, especially with a life-threatening disease, stop waiting for God to heal you.

"Well," you might say, "I'll just keep going to church and Sunday school and trust the Lord to heal me when He gets ready."

Go ahead. And before long, we'll order flowers for your casket. We'll bury your body. But if you pay attention as you read this book, you'll find out that you have power in Jesus' name over all devils and their work.

So, resist the Devil in the name of Jesus.

"Well, I was hoping the Lord would help me," you say. "This devil has been bothering me for *years.*"

Do you know why? Because you've been *ignorant* for years. Why don't you resist that dumb devil that's following you around?

"Well, Brother Norvel, I've *tried* to."

Well, that's your problem. You've got to be kidding. You don't *try* to resist the Devil. You just do it. Resist him with authority. Say that word out loud: *authority.*

Use the Name of Jesus

"I believe in the blood of Jesus, Brother Norvel," you say. "I'm born again by the Spirit of the Lord. And I believe all power is in Jesus' name."

But you also say, "Now, Devil, I really wish you'd stop trying to make me take drugs. I want to take drugs so much that I can hardly stand it. But I'm born again, Devil. I believe Jesus is real and I believe in His blood. So Devil, I wish you'd please leave me alone. I feel so bad. Please leave me alone, Devil."

You can go on like that until you're blue in the face and nothing will change. Because that isn't resisting the Devil.

If that's all you do, you know, kindly ask the Devil to leave you alone, a devil will go to church with you and sit beside you. If you say, "I believe there's *power* in the blood of Jesus," that devil will say, "so do I." If you say, "I believe there's *power* in the name of Jesus," he will say, "I believe that, too!"

There *is* power in the name and blood of Jesus. But it's not enough to believe *that* power is there. Just believing that doesn't bring victory to your life. You have to *use* the name of Jesus against the Devil and his works.

And you must use Jesus' name with *authority*. You can't deal with the works of hell without authority. It won't work. You must speak with authority to get rid of the Devil and his works. That's all he listens to.

You need to say with authority, "Look, cancer, you're an invader. Get off of my body *in Jesus' name! Get out!* You can't kill me. No cancer will ever kill me. I bind you in Jesus' name. I *resist* you! Are you still here, cancer? I said *go!*"

Do that four or five times a day, every day. And when you're not doing that, worship the Lord sweetly, and softly. Sing a song to Jesus. Thank the Lord for healing you. Always approach Him with reverence, thanksgiving and appreciation for who He is and what He's done.

Then after you finish talking with God and ministering to Him, go back to dealing with the Devil, glory to God. Don't ever approach *him* reverently. Approach him with authority.

The Devil will encourage you to believe anything that keeps you from walking in victory over him. He will do anything he can to hurt you. He'll try to send your children to hell. He'll try to make them backslide and start taking drugs. He'll try to convince them to live with someone outside of marriage. He'll do anything he can get away with.

But you don't have to let him do any of that. You can bind up all devils in Jesus' name.

If It's Bad, It's From the Devil

Sometimes people get discouraged and are tempted to backslide because devils buffet them so much. If that's you, don't let those devils discourage you. Bind them in Jesus' name!

"Well, Brother Norvel," you say, "I would bind up the devil if I had one, but I don't have any devils."

Is that right? Listen, my dear, sweet, sanctified Christian friend, anything that's trying to mess up your life is from the Devil. Oh, yeah. The Devil tricks Christians all the time. He won't come to your house every morning wearing a sign that says, "I'm Satan and I'm a terror. I used to be beautiful, powerful, and lived in heaven as one of God's chief angels. But I've lost all that. And now I'm here to wreck your life."

No, the Devil won't tell you that. He'll just stay hidden and give you a headache. You'll wake up and say, "Oh, this is a bad headache! My head is pounding! I'd better not go to church today."

If anything is wrong with you when you wake up, it's from the Devil. Just tell him, "Oh no you don't, Satan. You're not putting this on *me*. I don't receive it. I *resist* you in Jesus' name! I break your power. I bind you!"

"But Brother Norvel," you say, "what if I do that five or six times and the headache doesn't leave? What then, Brother Norvel?"

Just keep on doing it. Keep saying, "I resist you in Jesus' name. Get off of me!" If you do that long enough, that headache will leave.

The gospel of the Lord Jesus Christ doesn't work part-time. If you obey what Jesus tells you to do, I guarantee that whatever the Devil is bothering you with will leave. It will disappear!

You Have the Authority

You can take authority over evil spirits, my friend, because you're born again and the Holy Spirit lives in you. If you believe in Jesus, you have the authority to use His name. The name of Jesus has authority and power over all devils, diseases, heartaches, sadness and loneliness.

If you believe Jesus Christ is the Son of God, and you have confessed Him as your Savior and Lord, I guarantee that you can take authority over any devil and make it leave. Resist! One word: Resist!

Think about the words, "authority over devils." Christians sometimes forget who they are. They don't forget who *Jesus* is. If they're saved and live right, they know who *He* is. And they need to remember who He is, because His name will take them to heaven.

But too many Christians, bless their sweet hearts, love the Lord but forget who *they* are.

You're not just another person living on Spruce Street or Maple Avenue. Your name is written in *heaven*. You are a citizen of heaven, where there are no devils, thank God. In heaven there are no diseased, crippled or heartbroken people, no drunks, no drug addicts and no killers. Heaven is full of peace and joy. And if you want to know the truth about it, it would be fine with me if I was there right now.

You Can Do It

I want you to know without a doubt, my friend, that *you* can cast out devils. It's not enough that *I* know how to do it. I can cast out devils for hours. For me, casting out a devil is as much a part of my life as taking a drink of water or eating a meal. I like to make devils leave people. The Lord taught me years ago how to do it.

But I want *other* people to know for themselves how to make a devil leave. *You* can make it leave. You don't need me to do it for you. You just think you do. I'll teach you how to cast out a devil.

Look very closely in this passage at what Jesus said to you:

And he said unto them, Go ye into all the world, and preach the gospel to every creature. He that believeth and is baptized shall be saved; but he that believeth not shall be damned.

Mark 16:15,16

Look at that! "He that believeth" means me! And it means you, too. Jesus said if you believe the gospel, you'll be saved. And when you believe in Him, look in verse 17 at what is supposed to happen.

And these signs shall follow them that believe; In my name shall they cast out devils....

"In My name," Jesus said. Say this out loud where you're reading: *Jesus' name is the greatest name on earth. It will get me to heaven. It will keep me free from devils.*

Jesus said, **In my name shall** *they* **cast out devils.**

"Hey, Brother Norvel," you might say, "*'they'* means *me!* That's me right there!"

That's right. Jesus is talking about you, and everyone else who believes in Him. He's saying that those who believe in Him shall use His name to cast out devils.

Now, maybe you have never cast a devil out of anybody. But if you had obeyed the Lord, you would have.

Go to a church where people obey Jesus. If you don't, you'll end up doing nothing. Because Jesus said, **...without me ye can do nothing** (John 15:5). He also said, **Why call ye me, Lord, Lord, and do not the things which I say?** (Luke 6:46.)

Your church may preach a message of salvation. That's great. But if that's the only message you have, you won't teach people anything more. You're leaving out all the rest of God's benefits.

God wants you to know about all of His benefits. As a believer in Jesus, you have a right to everything He has promised you. *All* of God's promises belong to you and your family. And the first benefit Jesus promised those who believe in Him in Mark 16:17 and 18 is the right to use His name to cast out devils.

Jesus' first disciples exercised authority over devils in His name.

And the seventy returned again with joy, saying, Lord, even the devils are subject unto us through thy name.

Luke 10:17

Jesus wants believers today to exercise that same authority. If you're born again, don't be afraid to say, "In Jesus' name, devil, *come out!* In Jesus' name, you cancer, I break your power over this body. *Come out* I said! I curse your roots! *Come out!*"

Many times — not every time, but many times — that devil will come out right away. Cancer will just disappear.

Jesus' name is powerful enough to make things disappear. Jesus' name eats cancers for breakfast, blessed be God forever!

"Where did the cancer devil go?" you might ask.

I don't know, and I don't care.

When my daughter Zona was a little girl, I cursed growths on her body, and when they disappeared, she asked me the same question.

"Daddy, where did they go to? I can't find them anywhere," she asked when Jesus set her free.

"Give me a break, honey," I answered. "I don't want you to find them. I've looked at those ugly things too long."

"But Daddy, I want to know where they went. I count those growths every day. Where did they go to, Daddy?"

"I don't know where they went. And the rest of them have to leave, too. They don't have any choice."

"Oh, they don't?"

"*No,* because you belong to me and I'm not giving them any choice. They can't stay in your body."

Jesus had already told me that He thought I was crazy for leaving those growths on my daughter's body for five years. When He talked to me about them, I told Him that I'd been asking *Him* all that time to remove them. He seemed surprised when I said that.

I thought I was supposed to ask *God* to remove those growths. I thought *He* was supposed to do it. I prayed for five years, but the more I prayed, the bigger those ugly things got. (That's a sign you aren't getting anywhere.)

Then one night Jesus straightened me out. He took me up into His presence in the heavenlies and talked to me. That scared me so much I couldn't speak. I was trembling with holy awe. If you ever come into God's presence in the holy of holies, you'll be scared, too, glory to God.

Jesus thought I was stupid. (If you want to know the truth about it, He didn't *think* I was stupid. He *knew* I was.)

"How long are you going to put up with those growths on your daughter's body?" He asked. "Why don't you curse those growths in My name? Curse the roots of those growths in My name and they will die and disappear, if you will believe and not doubt. Do it by faith, son. By faith, *you* must do it. By faith, *you* must do it."

I came back down to earth and re-entered my body. In a few minutes, my physical senses began to return.

After that, I'm telling you, I cursed those growths in Jesus' name! Then for the next forty days and nights I *thanked* the Lord for removing them. At the end of that time, those growths totally disappeared from my daughter's back. And God gave her new skin just like He did for Naaman the leper. (2 Kings 5:1-14.)

You Take Authority

"Brother Norvel," you say, "my daughter has growths like that. Her body is deformed. She's been that way for a long time. The Lord hasn't done anything about it and I don't think He ever will."

Well now, if that's what you think, you might as well save your breath. You can't tell me the Lord Jesus Christ won't make your deformed child normal. You can't tell me that He won't wipe *all* growths away and create new skin over your child's entire body in a matter of seconds. You may convince somebody else that Jesus won't do that, but you can't convince me. You're too late! He's already been to my house! He's been there and left my daughter with no growths and new skin. *Glory to God forevermore!*

But God won't do anything about *your* daughter's deformed body until *you* do. Until you take authority in Jesus' name over those deformities, your child will stay like that. *You,* my brother, must make the Devil leave. You, my sister, must make the Devil leave.

Decide that you want something changed. Claim it in Jesus' name, by faith. Then, thank God continually for it. When you do these things, get ready, because God is on His way to your house.

Use Jesus' name to curse whatever the Devil tries to do in your life. Remember, Jesus said, **In my name shall they** [believers] **cast out devils...** (Mark 16:17). Say it out loud: *In Jesus' name, I cast out devils.*

Settle it in your own mind and spirit right now! You are a believer, and you have authority over devils and diseases in Jesus' name.

It's in the Bible

Do what Jesus tells you to do. I'm not teaching you anything that's not in the Bible. If He gave authority over devils to His early disciples, He will also give it to you.

Then he called his twelve disciples together, and gave them power and authority over all devils, and to cure diseases.

Luke 9:1

Jesus gave His disciples power and authority over *all* devils, not just a few weak ones. He gave them authority over lupus, cancer, crippled legs and any other damage the Devil wants to do.

You can have all the authority in the world, though, and it won't do you any good unless you exercise it. You must exercise your rights in Christ Jesus with the authority of *faith*, and a strong voice, in Jesus' name.

When you come against a deadly disease or any other work of the Devil, say, "In Jesus' name, I set my eyes like flint toward heaven and I will not detour. I will not weaken. I will not — *I will not* — take defeat for an answer. No. I take *victory* — victory in Jesus' name! I take authority over this in Jesus' name."

Miraculous May

If my friend May Stafford hadn't learned how to use the name of Jesus against the Devil, she would have died years ago. Her healing testimony will show you that God will do anything for people.

In 1976, May was at a Sunday morning service in Pensacola, Florida, where I was speaking to about a thousand people. She was confined to a wheelchair, suffering with four or five incurable, fatal diseases. She was fifty-eight years old but she looked about ninety-five. Cerebral palsy had crippled and twisted her body so much that her internal organs were out of place.

May could talk about Jesus, but her mind was mostly gone. She had lived in a nursing home for three years, sleeping in a bed fitted with metal bars to keep her from falling out. She had worn glasses for forty-five years and was legally blind.

In my sermon that morning, I was firing away from Matthew 16, and at one point I asked, "Why don't we in the church let God be God?"

All of a sudden, God said to me, "Yeah, that's right, son. Why don't you let Me be God? Touch that woman right there in that wheelchair."

I thought He wanted me to lay hands on her and pray for her. So I walked down to where she sat and started to do that, and the split second the end of my finger touched her, she seemed to disappear. I mean, the wheelchair was empty.

"My God," I thought, "that was a strong prayer! I didn't even pray! Where did she go to?"

Suddenly, the pastor and congregation started yelling. May was on the other side of the church running around in circles screaming "Jesus!" The Lord gave her perfect vision. Her mind returned, her body straightened out and her feet and hands became totally normal, glory to God forever!

May said later that she didn't remember anything about what happened when I touched her. She went blank.

Medical Science Couldn't Help

Now, when you leave the nursing home where you live in the morning crippled and in a wheelchair, and you return that afternoon pushing your wheelchair and walking normally, people there want to know where you've been.

So when they asked, May told them, "I've been to church, glory to God forever!"

"You've been to *church*, May?" they asked, amazed.

"Yes! I've been to *church*, blessed be the name of the Lord forever! Thank You, Jesus! Thank You, Jesus!" Then she started speaking in other tongues.

That night, the registered nurse who had cared for May Stafford came to our evening service. She stood up and said, "People, I know medical science, and nothing connected with it could help this woman. I've been her nurse for over three years and I'm telling you that medical science couldn't help her eyes, her mind, her spirit, her crippled body or anything else that was wrong with her. Almighty God has done this for her."

Now, to be honest, I'd never heard of the Lord healing anyone like that before. It was the greatest miracle I'd ever seen. What shocked me the most, though, was that God restored some of May's youth. The woman I saw running around in circles screaming "Jesus!" didn't look like the same woman who was sitting in the wheelchair I walked over to. She looked much younger.

During the months that followed, May Stafford heard this same teaching about believers' authority over the Devil that you're reading now. She put it into practice, and the Lord eventually called her into a healing and miracle ministry.

Sixteen years after the Lord miraculously healed her, this woman, at age seventy-four, was traveling around the United States holding healing meetings and seeing the Lord work miracles.

The Devil keeps trying to kill May, but she knows the authority she has in Jesus' name and just resists him. She resists him! May tells him, "Devil, you know you're not going to do this." And she walks in the joy of the Lord.

God Still Performs Miracles

Honestly, I can't think of a Pentecostal church in the world that believes Jesus will pick up a crippled woman during a service, shoot her through the air, straighten out her bones and give her perfect eyesight and a new mind. Do you know any church that believes that?

Members in the average Pentecostal church would say, "I never saw God do anything like that in *this* church."

Well, I had never seen God do anything like that, either. But I saw Him do it that morning. And, as they say, "The proof of the pudding is in the eating."

When I see God do something I don't expect, it takes me out of my little world, and I learn from it.

This woman was legally blind. She couldn't see me. Her mind was gone. She didn't even know what I spoke in that service. Her body was twisted and crippled. Medical science gave her no hope. And God healed her.

Now, think about it, friend. God says, **I am the Lord, I change not...** (Malachi 3:6). He never changes. So if He healed one person like that, He will heal anybody. If He healed then, He will heal now.

Do you know why we don't receive more miracles from God? We don't expect them. When we ask God for something He has promised us in His Word, we need to *expect* Him to do it for us.

God tells us in the Bible that healing is one of His benefits:

> **Bless the Lord, O my soul, and forget not all his benefits: Who forgiveth all thine iniquities;** *who healeth all thy diseases.*
>
> **Psalm 103:2,3**

That's what God did for May. He healed *all* her diseases.

Another Miracle

May Stafford told me about another miracle the Lord worked for her when she was seventy-five years old.

Now understand, when you reach a certain age, bags and wrinkles start appearing under your eyes. And that happened to May.

One day, as she looked at her face in a mirror, she said, "I'm not going to accept these wrinkles. They're getting too big. Lord, I don't want these wrinkles under my eyes. I take *authority* over these wrinkles in Jesus' name!" And as she watched, all those wrinkles disappeared. God just smoothed them away!

"Brother Norvel," you say, "is that really the truth? Does God make people younger?"

Yes, He does. It's another one of His benefits spoken of in Psalm 103:5:

Who satisfieth thy mouth with good things; *so that thy youth is renewed like the eagle's.*

When May Stafford was seventy-five, God renewed her youth! He smoothed away those wrinkles.

When you hear what God did for May Stafford, it's enough to convince you to pack all your clothes in a suitcase and go live in church! It makes you want to just live there and compel people who are crippled or have any other problem to get in a service so the Lord can heal them. I tell you, the hand of the Lord — the Spirit of the living God — is available for the *church!*

Authority Over Demon Possession

Remember, Jesus gave His disciples **power and authority over *all* devils, and to cure diseases** (Luke 9:1). So believers have power and authority over *all* devils and diseases, not just some.

103

The Spirit of the Lord told me one day in a shopping center in the city where I live to go to a certain address in another city in that same state. So I obeyed, and there, on a college campus, I found a demon-possessed student.

In those days, streaking was a popular college prank. Streakers took off their clothes and ran naked across campus. And this young man, who had been a sharp student, got involved with streaking and lost his mind. It just snapped, and he became a total vegetable. He was about twenty-one years old and didn't even know his own name.

Now remember this. It will help you. What you *do* with your *body* affects your *mind*. If you do godly things with your body, you give God room to work in your mind. But if you do demonic things with your body, you give the Devil room to work in your mind.

I walked into the building where this student was being cared for and met the college psychiatrist. The psychiatrist asked me to pray for the young man.

"I'll pray for him," I said, "as long as you stay out of the room and leave me here alone with him."

"But we want to stay in here and watch him," the psychiatrist said. "Mr. Hayes, a year ago I didn't even believe in what you do. But I heard a man on television say that you and Lester Sumrall cast the devil out of him.

"At least I've been reading books about this," he continued. "Now I believe in it. And now I have this case. This young man doesn't even know his own name."

The psychiatrist introduced us, but the student wouldn't say a word. He just sat still in a chair.

I told the psychiatrist and the other doctors with him to leave and stay out.

After they left the room, I walked up to the student, laid my hands on him and said, "Father, in Jesus' name I bring this boy before You right now. And Satan, I want to serve you notice. The Lord God moved upon me and told me to come here. And so, *I've come to get this boy's mind back for him.*

"Now, I know you want to keep this mind. You'd like to put this young man in a mental institution for the rest of his life, because that's the closest thing you have to hell on earth. But this young man is not going to a mental institution, because God has sent me here to get his mind back for him.

"In Jesus' name, Satan, I command you to obey me. I bind you in Jesus' name. *Come out of him!* I command you to obey me in the name of the Lord Jesus Christ. *Come out of him, I said!* Turn him loose on the inside. I reach way down deep on the inside of this young man and I grab hold of you, Satan, and I *pull you out of there!* I command you, *come out of him and leave him alone!"*

Then I laid my hands on that student's head and said, "I command his *mind* to come back into him and to function normally." And I went on like that for probably thirty minutes, until my body and my voice started tiring.

Always remember: Don't let devils wear you out. People who let devils wear them out don't know what they're doing.

"But you said you were tired, so what did you do?" you ask.

What do you think I did? What are you supposed to do when you get tired? I sat down in a chair and rested.

That young man just sat there. He hadn't made a noise. He didn't move, not a flinch; nothing.

So I sat resting in that chair for about half an hour. Oh, maybe every five or ten minutes I'd sit up and say, "Are you still trying to possess him, devil? I told you to come out!"

Then, once I was good and rested, I stood up and began speaking the same way I had before to that devil. I walked over to the young man and said, "In Jesus' name, *come out of him!* You can't have him! You can't have this mind in Jesus' name. *Come out of him, I said!*"

After a while, I grew tired again. So I walked over to the chair, sat down and rested some more.

After about an hour, as I sat resting, the young man stood up and walked to the other end of that long room. (Until then, he hadn't said a word or made a move.) He walked as far away from me as he could. Then he lay down on the floor in a corner and started barking like a dog.

You know, I thought, *I've been in the ministry for years, and devils are weird.* Every one of them is different. You could cast out devils for a hundred years and still run into one and say, "I haven't ever seen anything like *this* before."

Well, the young man stopped barking. Then he started shouting, "Water! Water! I want water! Water!" Then he went back to barking again.

Oh brother, I thought. Devils always want water for some reason.

Suddenly, the door flew open and in raced the psychiatrist like an English butler carrying a big pitcher of water. His helper was right behind him.

"No you don't," I said. "Where are you going?"

"Well," the psychiatrist said, "I'm going to, uh, uh.... Well, we were downstairs and heard him yelling for water. So we came to give him a drink."

"Give him a drink?" I asked. "I don't give the devil any drinks." (Give me a break! When you want to bury a devil and you give him a drink, in a few minutes he'll ask for a cheeseburger and french fries!)

"Oh," said the psychiatrist, "so you're not going to give him a drink?"

"No. I don't obey devils."

"Uh, it was devils that wanted a drink?"

"Yes. It was devils."

"Oh. I thought it was him."

"No. Now you two leave and don't come back."

Then the psychiatrist and his helper left.

Now, I'm teaching you a valuable lesson about casting out devils in this chapter. So, you need to have ears to hear. I just kept speaking by faith. "In Jesus' name, *come out of him,* I said, and leave him alone! I command this young man's mind to come back into him. In Jesus' name, *come out of him!*"

You need to speak with a voice of authority, in Jesus' name.

Perseverance Makes the Difference

I kept that up all night long. That's what makes the difference. That's where you separate the men from the boys.

Always remember: You can hear from God any time you want to, about anything, if you'll pay the price. Peter was delivered by angels because a prayer group was willing to pay the price.

Peter therefore was kept in prison: but prayer was made *without ceasing* of the church unto God for him.

Acts 12:5

It wasn't easy to get Peter out of jail. But it happened because the church — notice Scripture says "the church" — prayed *without ceasing* to God for him. ·

Peter was being held in a jail cell behind locked iron gates. You can't get through locked gates. There's no way. And as if that wasn't enough, the Bible says, **...Peter was sleeping between two soldiers, bound with two chains: and the keepers before the door kept the prison** (Acts 12:6).

Peter was bound with chains and under constant guard. Naturally speaking, escape was impossible.

But because the church persisted in prayer for Peter, God sent an angel to free him.

Don't ever worry about how God will do something. He isn't limited to natural means.

And He has ears to hear. He is a faith God. So when you show God your faith — when you act on what you believe — He responds. He responded to the prayers of the church and brought Peter out of jail.

Faith Brings Results

I rebuked the devil in that young man all night long, in basically the same way. When I grew tired, I sat down and rested, then started again. I did it by faith, and in Jesus' name.

About daybreak, as I sat resting, the young man stood up. Until then, all he had done was bark like a dog and ask for water. Then he walked over in front of me, stopped, lifted a leg and just stood there.

Well, he'll last about five minutes, I thought.

I kept watching him, but he didn't flinch. He just stood there with one leg up and his face in front of mine.

"In Jesus' name, *come out of him,*" I said. "I told you yesterday, come out of him. I'm telling you today, come out of him. You have no choice. You can't stay in him because I'm not going to let you. You're not going to get this boy's mind, because I've come to get it back for him. In Jesus' name, *come out of him!*"

The young man didn't move. He didn't say a word. He just stood there on one foot.

After about thirty minutes of that, his lips parted and the tip of his tongue stuck out a tiny bit.

I've been looking at this guy all night, I thought, *and this is different. What's he doing this for? He's changed.*

"In Jesus' name, *come out of him!*" I said again. After I said that a few more times, the young man's tongue stuck out a little farther. I told him four or five more times, and it came out a little more. In a little while, his tongue was sticking way out and he opened his mouth wide.

There that young man stood, on one leg, his tongue sticking out and his mouth wide open. Weird. I'm telling you devils are weird.

I just kept on. "In Jesus' name, *come out of him, I said!* Turn this man loose!"I was doing this by faith because God told me to go there. If you have the Holy Ghost in you, you have authority.

Then all of a sudden, I noticed a kind of white-looking saliva oozing out from one side of his tongue. It wasn't spittle and it didn't run. It moved slowly, like lava from a Hawaiian volcano, stringing down from his tongue, hanging. It wouldn't fall.

Then, more of that white-looking stuff started oozing from the other side of the young man's tongue.

I didn't change what I was doing. "In Jesus' name, come out of him, I said!" I had been saying that for hours.

You don't have to change what you're doing. Just obey Jesus. Don't throw a fit, scream or turn flips. Be steadfast and unmovable and keep commanding the devil in Jesus' name to leave.

"In Jesus' name, *come out of him, I said!* I told you all night, you can't have his mind. I'm not going to let you. In Jesus' name, *come out of him!*"

That white stuff streaming down from the young man's tongue started making a puddle on the floor. And all this time, he was still standing on one foot.

"In Jesus' name, *come out of him, I said!* I claim this boy's mind."

Now, remember the Bible story about Lot's wife turning into a pillar of salt? (See Genesis 19:26.) This young man froze just like that. I mean, he froze solid. A whole puddle of that white-looking, stringy saliva was oozing out of his mouth making a puddle on the floor. And when it stopped running, he was as stiff as a board, frozen like a statue.

It was then that I called for help, and four of us picked that young man up. He didn't move a muscle. His legs stayed in the same position they were in while he stood on one foot. We carried him into another room and put him to bed.

Now, it's not easy to cover a guy with a sheet and a blanket when one leg is sticking way up and he's stiff as a board. But somehow we managed to cover him up, leg and all. He was frozen just like a piece of ice — just like a glass statue. His whole body was hard and stiff. His fingers didn't even feel like fingers.

But after that young man slept for a little while, he woke up totally normal, glory to God! His mind had snapped back into him, because the Devil had to go in Jesus' name!

Maintaining Deliverance

College officials called the young man's father in a distant state, and the father came to take his son home.

"I want to thank you for praying for my son, Mr. Hayes," the father said to me. "The people here told me that you prayed for him all night long."

"Yes, I did," I said. "Somebody had to do it, sir, and God sent me down here. I knew that if I didn't pray for your son, he would spend the rest of his life in a mental institution. He didn't even know his own name."

Now get this: When devils get that strong a grip on you, they won't turn you loose. Whoever they have will stay under their control for the rest of their life unless somebody prays and breaks their power. And God's power to cast them out is available in Jesus' name! It's available for *you*. It's available for me.

The young man's father asked me what I thought he should do now to help his son.

"Sir," I said, "you'd better find him a believing church. Now, what kind of church do you go to?"

"I go to a Bible-believing church," he said.

"Well, they all believe in the Bible," I said. "But in a true full-gospel, Bible believing church, a person needs to be able to leave his seat, walk over to the pastor and kneel down before God. A person needs to be able to say, 'Pastor, the Devil is attacking my body with sickness. Please make this devil leave me, and lay your hands on me in Jesus' name so I can be healed.' Do they do that at your church?"

"No," he answered, "I don't think my pastor knows anything about that."

"Then you had better find another church. Don't take your son back to that church, because those devils will try to come back on him. And if you don't know your authority as a believer in Jesus, you'd better find somebody who does.

Sir, take your son to a Bible-believing church where the pastor believes in healing, miracles, the laying on of hands and authority in Jesus' name. Go to a church where the pastor knows how to cast out devils. If you don't find a pastor who can help you like that, those devils will come back and take your son over again. Don't let them. Resist them in Jesus' name."

Then I told him to look for a full-gospel church. Those are the only ones who may have pastors who know about what I was telling him. "But you have to check up on those churches, too," I said, "because some of them don't believe right, either."

I continued, "Before you start attending a church regularly, ask the pastor, 'Do you believe in being born again?' If he says yes, ask him, 'Do you believe in the laying on of hands and in Jesus healing sick people today?" If that pastor mumbles and sounds negative, just say, "Thank you very much. I won't see you later, alligator. I won't bother you anymore."

The laying on of hands is a doctrine of the New Testament church. And if you change a doctrine of the church, you won't have the Lord's power. Now, you'll still be saved. You won't be in trouble with Jesus, because He loves you. But you won't have His *power*.

One Word: Resist

When you change doctrines of the New Testament church, you lose the power of God. Don't change sound doctrines. Stay steadfast in Jesus' name, and His power will come. Remember, one word: Resist.

Take authority over devils. Resist them in Jesus' name. God's power will come to you by faith. You don't have to be in a revival-type meeting, sing three songs and listen to four sermons before God will show His power. You don't have to run around doing this and that. You simply have to *resist*.

God can send you, by yourself, late in the evening to a house in another city. You can walk in with no singing, no praying, no Bible — nothing except Jesus' name. And

113

when you speak that name with authority, you can cast the devil out of a demon-possessed person.

You can say, "In Jesus' name, devil, let him go! *Come out, I said!* Turn this person loose! In Jesus' name, *come out!*" And don't stop doing that until the devil comes out. Don't let your faith waver. Speak to devils in Jesus' name with authority and watch what God does for you.

You'll break the devil's power loose from that person in Jesus' name. You can break cancer loose from your own body once you know how. Just say, "No you don't, cancer. Uh-uh. No. In Jesus' name you're not going to kill me. *Come out of me, I said!*"

Just do that boldly until the cancer lets go. And if you do it long enough, cancer *will* let go.

I exercise authority over the Devil that way, and I guarantee that you can do it, too. You will find God's destiny for you and walk in it when you learn to resist, and you'll help many others too.

Now let's take a close look at the importance of love in Chapter 6.

—6—

Love

When writing a book about Christian destiny, the main thing that should be said is our ultimate destiny is to be more like God. And God is love. So as I said earlier in Chapter 1, right away we should see how important it is to love. But we don't want the Devil to have open season on us, so we need to obey God's protecting commandments so we can bless the world with His love. Let's look at the great love commandment now in Matthew 22:

> When the Pharisees had heard that he had put the Sadducees to silence, they were gathered together. Then one of them, which was a lawyer, asked him a question, tempting him, and saying, Master, which is the great commandment in the law? Jesus said unto him, Thou shalt love the Lord thy God with all thy heart, and with all thy soul, and with all thy mind. This is the first and great commandment.
>
> Matthew 22:34-38

Worship God

In this passage, Jesus teaches us to worship God with all of our heart, soul and mind. See, if you love your God then you will worship Him. If you don't worship God, you can love Him with your own version of love, but it won't bring heaven's dividends to you.

"But Brother Norvel, I don't ever worship God in a room alone," you say, "and I love Him."

Well, you love God at a distance. You love Him with your own version of love.

Always remember: Your version doesn't count. God will not approve of your version of love. He approves of what Jesus said to do. And Jesus called worshiping God and loving Him with your heart, mind and soul, the first and great commandment. This is in the Old Testament in Exodus 20:3, where God said, **Thou shalt have no other gods before me.**

Love Your Neighbor

After Jesus told that Pharisee lawyer the great commandment, He gave him the second greatest commandment:

And the second is like unto it, Thou shalt love thy neighbour as thyself. On these two commandments hang all the law and the prophets
Matthew 22:39,40

Now I want you to think about that. All that the Old Testament prophets ever said, and all of the Old Testament Law, is summed up in these two commandments.

So in everyday language, the way you treat God and human beings determines whether the Bible works for you.

I'll boil it down. If you obey Jesus — if you do what Jesus told the lawyer and put first things first — diseases will begin to disappear from your body. Everything about you will start to change.

116

Bow down before God. Worship and love Him with all your heart, mind and soul. And love your neighbor as you love yourself. You can't love God and hate the world.

The Lord let me know a long time ago that if people don't obey Him in these things, the destiny He has for them will never be theirs.

How Are We Able To Love?

Jesus told us to love the Lord our God and to love our neighbors as ourselves. And if He told us to do it — we can do it! Jesus knows what He is doing. These commandments are given in the correct order. The first commandment is to love the Lord our God. So we have to do that first before we are able to do the second commandment, loving our neighbor as ourselves.

The Bible says, **We love him, because he first loved us** (1 John 4:19).

So Jesus showed us how to love through the deeds of His life.

Now let's back up a couple of verses in 1 John and see how we'll be able to love our neighbor.

Whosoever shall confess that Jesus is the Son of God, God dwelleth in him, and he in God. And we have known and believed the love that God hath to us. God is love; and he that dwelleth in love dwelleth in God, and God in him. Herein is our love made perfect, that we may have boldness in the day of judgment: because as he is, so are we in this world.

1 John 4:15-17

117

Now we can know that it is God dwelling in us and us dwelling in Him that makes us able to love. So Jesus not only showed us, but He came to dwell in us to help us love.

We are able to love our neighbor because, **the love of God is shed abroad in our hearts by the Holy Ghost which is given unto us** (Romans 5:5).

And because the Holy Spirit lives in us, we have His fruits: His fruits of love. **But the fruit of the Spirit is love, joy, peace, longsuffering, gentleness, goodness, faith, meekness, temperance...** (Galatians 5:22, 23).

Have Mercy

What kind of spirit do you have in you? The kind I have in me wants to have mercy on beaten-down people. They need help. When the Devil tricks and messes up whole families, I want to have mercy on them. I hate the Devil for doing those things.

I don't care how good, or strong you are in faith. If you don't obey the Lord Jesus and "love thy neighbor as thyself," you're in trouble with God. He will still bless you, but He won't let you have His greatest blessings.

Jesus is a rewarder, so He said you can't give somebody a cup of cold water without receiving a reward from Him for doing it. (Matthew 10:40-42.) If God will reward you for such a small act, imagine what He will do if you really help somebody.

God is in the rewarding business. He wants to reward you because He loves you so much.

...Verily I say unto you, Inasmuch as ye have done it unto one of the least of these my brethren, ye have done it unto me.

Matthew 25:40

118

Get this: When we *help* people, we *reward* the Lord. We give something to God when we do something for somebody else. Buy a hungry person some food and God will reward you!

Jesus told me to love my neighbor as I love myself. The neighbor He was talking about is anyone who needs help, not necessarily the person who lives next door.

Forgive and Be Forgiven

When I sin and ask God to forgive me, I want Him to forgive me. So when my neighbor sins, I should forgive him. Jesus said:

If ye forgive men their trespasses, your heavenly Father will also forgive you: But if ye forgive not men their trespasses, neither will your Father forgive your trespasses.

Matthew 6:14,15

I thank God for forgiving me of many sins. And because He has, I know I must show mercy, compassion and love to my neighbor when he sins if I want God to keep on forgiving me.

In another Scripture, Jesus said, **By this shall all men know that ye are my disciples, if ye have love one to another** (John 13:35). If unbelievers see Christians fight with each other and act mean just like people in the world, why would they want to become Christians?

Look. If you're going to follow God Almighty, I have news for you. When you were born again, you gave up all of your rights except one. The only right you have is to be nice. Did you get that? God saved you to be nice and to love the brethren.

Now I'm not talking about ignoring someone who is causing a real problem that you've already warned three times and he won't stop. Jesus told us how to love in this situation:

> **Moreover if thy brother shall trespass against thee, go and tell him his fault between thee and him alone: if he shall hear thee, thou hast gained thy brother. But if he will not hear thee, then take with thee one or two more, that in the mouth of two or three witnesses every word may be established. And if he shall neglect to hear them, tell it unto the church: but if he neglect to hear the church, let him be unto thee as an heathen man and a publican.**
>
> **Matthew 18:15-17**

This Scripture says to warn sinning brothers three times. Then, if they still won't listen to you, throw them out and don't have any more to do with them. But you have to go to them at least three times. And, you have to go in God's compassionate love.

Don't Disagree With God

It's not God's will for me to run you down with my words and destroy your name or cause you heartaches and trouble over some sin you committed a long time ago.

"Why, he used to take drugs," someone might say of a brother. "I won't have anything to do with him. He's a drug addict."

No, he's not. Jesus saved him. That brother stands before God washed white as snow with the blood of the Lamb. Haven't you ever read this scripture?

Therefore if any man be in Christ, he is a new creature: old things are passed away; behold, all things are become new. And all things are of God, who hath reconciled us to himself by Jesus Christ, and hath given to us the ministry of reconciliation.

2 Corinthians 5:17,18

So, you better watch it real closely about disagreeing with God. You can get into serious trouble. It doesn't matter what anyone has ever done. God wants to be your God and set you free.

"Well," you say, "if I see my neighbor doing something wrong, I'll tell on him. He shouldn't get away with that."

Yeah, sure. Maybe you can get by with that for a few years. But you'll suffer for treating a brother that way. God hasn't called you to hurt people. He has called you to love people, especially brokenhearted or weak people. He tells the strong to help the weak.

"You shall love your neighbor as yourself." How would you like God to send a couple of angels to your church service, have them put up a big screen, turn to you and say, "This is your life," and start showing everything you've ever done? There would be all of your past sins and how you did them. You wouldn't like that a bit.

Think of that the next time you're tempted to talk about a brother or sister who once sinned. No man has a right to expose another man's sins when God has forgiven him.

I don't have any right to act like your friend, let you tell me all the awful things you've been through, and then expose you. That's the best way I know of to die

121

young. God gets so disgusted with you that He just lets you die, you crazy thing, you.

Why does He let you die? Because you're a murderer. You murder people with your tongue. You take on an Absalom demon. Many people do that. They try to draw things away from another person and find favor for themselves (see 2 Samuel 15:1-6). And if you keep it up, a curse or disease will come upon you because you're a demon-follower.

Tricky Demons

Certain kinds of very tricky demons operate through Christians — preachers and Sunday school teachers — and they don't even know a demon is tricking them. It deceives them into thinking that they have the right to condemn Christian brothers and sisters for past sins.

We need to also pray for preachers who have stumbled publicly, and for denominations in trouble. If we all pray for them, God will work it out. He can restore them with His Word and His love in just a few days. God said, "I'll make the rough places smooth and the crooked places straight." (Isaiah 40:4, author's paraphrase.)

Restore a Brother or Sister

Brethren, if a man be overtaken in a fault, ye which are spiritual, restore such an one in the spirit of meekness; considering thyself, lest thou also be tempted.

Bear ye one another's burdens, and so fulfil the law of Christ.

For if a man think himself to be something, when he is nothing, he deceiveth himself.

Galatians 6:1-3

So for any of us who are ministering and daily seeking to live out God's destiny for our lives, we must learn to walk in love. We may know exactly what God wants us to do for Him. But if we don't love other people, especially our brothers and sisters in Jesus, we'll never achieve God's destiny for us.

When a brother or sister in the Lord does something wrong, love them. Don't expose them.

Some time ago, a man I know pioneered a church. His wife played the piano for services and he preached. Under his leadership, the church grew very large.

But then, suddenly, he and his wife took their two children, left that church and moved to another town.

Why?

While he was pastoring, the man had become involved with another woman in that church. But the people didn't know about it until after he left when that "other" woman grew angry because he left, and exposed him.

In the new town, the man took over as pastor of another church, and things went fine for a time. But then he got involved with a woman in the new church.

This time, his wife left him and took the children with her. And the man lost that pastorate, too.

After that, he took a job selling cars in Los Angeles for about two years. Now there's nothing wrong with selling cars. But this man was called to preach. The anointing of God was all over him.

I couldn't get him off of my mind. Then one day the Lord said to me, "He's a chosen vessel. Go restore him." So I went to Los Angeles and called him on the phone.

His new wife answered. "God wants me to talk to your husband," I said.

Even though I had never met her, she broke down and began to cry. "Oh, I am so glad that you called," she said. "It has to be God's will."

"You've got that right," I said. "If it wasn't, I wouldn't be calling. I have a direct order from God to talk to him and restore him. I didn't just come to talk."

"Oh," she said, "he's been like a fish out of water."

"I can imagine," I said. "As good a preacher as he is, he *must* be like a fish out of water."

So we picked a place and set a time to meet. When we got together, I asked him how much his new wife knew about him.

"She knows everything. Say anything you want to in front of her."

I said, "All right." So I began to talk and minister to him.

Here we were in a fancy restaurant and the glory of God fell on us. It hovered over the table and broke my friend. He began to weep. We all did. He poured his guts out about how lonely he had been.

That man needed to stay out there in a dry and lonely place for two years. I'd have gone to see him sooner, but it wasn't God's timing. He had pushed this thing twice. We serve a God Who is real, though, and He is willing to give us another chance.

Faced with another chance, he said, "No, Norvel. I can't do it."

"I know you can't," I said, "but the Holy Ghost can."

He kept saying, "I can't do it," but then God would melt him some more and he would just sob. The glory of God was all over the table. I mean, God wrung him out like a rag until he said, "I'll preach." Norvel Hayes didn't persuade him to say that. The Holy Ghost did.

I said, "Will you tell God right now in front of me that you'll never do anything like this again as long as you live?"

This former pastor had committed adultery twice on his ex-wife, and she and their two children lived in another state. And now, here he sat with a new wife. Who in the world would he minister to?

Well, Los Angeles is full of people with problems. He could minister to people with problems like he had. Some of them have had five or more spouses.

Apparently he had been trying to teach the Bible a little bit in his home. He had five or six couples who had been in trouble come to him. They asked him if he knew something about God. He said, "Yeah, I used to be a pastor." And because he used to be a preacher and they thought he was so kind and nice, they wanted him to teach them. So he had been having a private Bible study at his home.

I told him to keep holding those home meetings and to keep ministering to and strengthening those couples. And I told him to do that for others like them that he might find. Some of those couples had gone through such bad times they had been living in hell. Usually when your life gets to be in such a mess, nobody wants to have anything to do with you. But love will always reach out. Love will always restore.

There are many people the church wants nothing to do with. You have to watch the church. Sometimes they don't want to have anything to do with you if you don't dress well.

So this man obeyed the Lord. He kept on teaching these people. And now, he has had a church for a couple of years in Los Angeles. He is going along doing the best that he can.

I told him that his church would probably stay very small for a long time. I said that God would watch and expect the best of him, but that it would be a time before God's greatest blessings for that church could come. And they will, as he stays faithful to his pastoral call.

Tested Blessings

God has all kinds and sizes of blessings. He hopes that every person will grow to where he can receive His greatest blessings. But you need to pass some tests before God can release them to you.

Blessings come from God, not from someone else. And once you start receiving God's big blessings and everything works easier for you, no one will understand you. People will think you're weird, like me!

God enjoys blessing people. He has what the world is looking for. If you are sick and tired of living a shabby life, being confused and unhappy and not content, then seek Jesus. Turn your face toward heaven and tell Him you want Him. When you walk in God's love and make yourself a blessing to others, God will bless you with His expected end.

For I know the thoughts that I think toward you, saith the Lord, thoughts of peace, and not of

evil, to give you an expected end. Then shall ye call upon me, and ye shall go and pray unto me, and I will hearken unto you. And ye shall seek me, and find me, when ye shall search for me with all your heart.

Jeremiah 29:11-13

Those who diligently seek God shall find God. You can have anything you want from God. All you have to do is love, and seek Him until you get it. If you seek God the healer, you will find God the healer. If you seek God the joy-giver, you will find God the joy-giver.

If part of your life is empty and unsuccessful or needs building up, the Lord Jesus Christ can fix it. So seek Him. You can find God. He can restore like no one else can.

Restoration is for you and others. It is even for those who have had their failings shown in public.

God said we can show our love for Him when we obey His commandments. So you can show your love for God by the way you love the brethren. And you aren't loving the brethren when you want to expose them.

Can you imagine? Thousands of people won't have anything to do with religion or God or Jesus or the Bible. They'll go to hell because of what was exposed publicly.

Human beings aren't perfect. Sometimes the best, most powerful servants of God on earth blow it. Look in 2 Samuel 11:2-27 at what David did. Remember, he committed adultery and murder. His sin caused his son to die and a curse to come on his family. But he repented.

When one of God's servants blows it, don't be like a lot of people in the world. Don't turn against them, I beg of you. I don't care what they've done.

A lot of people make mistakes. And, yeah, God didn't create us to do those things. He didn't have anything to do with it. That's the work of hell — the work of the Devil.

But God is in the restoring business. If people repent and ask Him to forgive them, He will and so should you.

Love Your Pastor and the Church

Obey them that have the rule over you, and submit yourselves: for they watch for your souls, as they that must give account, that they may do it with joy, and not with grief: for that is unprofitable for you.

Hebrews 13:17

God not only wants you to show mercy to those who sin, He wants you to be merciful and compassionate to your pastor. Make sure that you love your pastor. Don't do anything against your pastor. If there is a problem, pray and let God handle it.

"But Brother Norvel," you say, "I think my pastor is doing an awful job."

Who cares what you think? That's God's business. Let Him take care of it.

Who art thou that judgest another man's servant? to his own master he standeth or falleth....

Romans 14:4

God has a book for you to go by. It's called the Bible. So read it and see how you're supposed to treat your pastor.

And while you're loving your pastor, love all churches. I love them all: Baptist, Methodist ... it doesn't matter.

You can show me the biggest church building in town with a beautiful sanctuary, parsonage and grounds. That church could sit on that expensive property all year and get just one soul saved and I would still believe in it.

I'd say, "Oh, don't ever tear it down. Keep it there." My God, in ten years they'd get ten souls saved. Jesus paid a great price for each and every soul.

I believe in all churches and denominations that preach Jesus. I just hate to see them cut themselves short from receiving from God Almighty. I can hardly believe most of their doctrines, but that's beside the point. If they preach Jesus and Him crucified, I think they ought to have a right to stay where they are and get people saved.

God so loved the world, and the sinners of the world, that He gave His only begotten Son. (See John 3:16.) God loves the sinners and the brethren. He has blessings for both of us. And if you'll obey what Jesus called the two greatest commandments in Matthew 22, God's blessings will fall on you all the time, and Satan will never be able to steal your destiny!

—7—

My Testimony

W*hen I gave my life to Jesus, I wasn't ready for Him to call me into the ministry. Some things in my life had to change before I could begin to walk in His divine destiny for me.*

I became successful in business as a young man. By the time I reached my late twenties I owned a manufacturing company and earned four or five thousand dollars a week.

My home sat on five acres surrounded by a big fence. A locked white gate between two marble posts kept people out whom I didn't want to see. A long driveway with large shrubs on each side wound toward the house through an acre of my perfectly manicured grounds.

Four Cadillac cars were parked in my garage. I didn't look like a movie star but I lived like one, with everything I could possibly want.

A men's club saved me a special seat. Doctors, lawyers and older fellows who owned manufacturing companies liked to sit and talk with me. I could fellowship with men from different professions of all ages.

Men twenty-five years older than me would ask my advice. It amazed me. There was something about the way I carried myself that they respected. I guess it was because I was so successful as a young man. I made more money than most of them.

Treated Like a King

I had a good marriage, too. My wife, Nona, was raised in Boston and was living in New York when we married. She treated me like a king. We lived together as man and wife for eleven years and had one child, Zona, our daughter.

Nona was raised Catholic and I was raised Baptist. So we agreed to never let religion wreck our home and went to our separate churches. But finally my wife grew tired of going to mass. She said she didn't get enough out of it and started coming to the Baptist church with me. She liked to hear the pastor preach.

I attended the First Baptist Church in Indianapolis, Indiana, with the rest of the rich men in town. It sure was different from the Southern Baptist church I grew up in back in Tennessee. There, everybody got down on the floor and prayed until God showed up, and then they'd shout all over the building! But in that First Baptist Church up north, nobody got down on the floor and prayed. When people get money and move uptown with the rich folks, they stop the shouting and the hours of praying on their knees before God.

Well, I should have had better sense than to go to that big-city church. My mother was an old-fashioned Southern Baptist. But you usually run with your own kind. If you're poor, you run with poor people. If you make four or five thousand dollars a week, you run with people who make that kind of money. Rich people usually go to a church where nothing is happening spiritually because that's what they want.

132

And that's just how I was. I didn't want anything spiritual happening. I just wanted to be a First Baptist businessman who acted real nice.

I wanted to put on my tailor-made suit, drive up in my Cadillac and sit on the pew in the most beautiful church in town. I'd sit there from eleven to twelve and listen to Dr. so-and-so give the announcements and Dr. such and such preach. Then I'd get up and run to my car. I didn't want anybody interfering with me or requiring anything of me.

Now I knew the pastor and some other people in that big-city church knew God, and were sincere. It was me who wasn't sincere. I wanted to be, but I had built a kingdom for myself. And I was trapped in it. I had authority over a great number of employees. That can affect your attitude. I felt I had to be the boss — separate from them, and always in charge.

I was the great, powerful boss. But when I looked in the mirror, I didn't like who I saw. Oh, I liked myself while I was driving in the busy traffic in Indianapolis, where we lived.

But when I thought back to Tennessee, where I was raised, I didn't like who I had become. Life there had been simple. In church, those old-fashioned Southern Baptist preachers ran up and down the aisles, and people prayed until God came on the scene.

But in the big city, I didn't care if the whole world went to hell. I didn't pass out a tract, knock on one door or do anything else for God. If my neighbor's house had burned down, I probably wouldn't have gone to visit.

My attitude was, "Leave me alone. I've got it made. Just let me go to church on Sunday morning and be a nice business executive."

Behind the fence on my estate, I'd sit and watch the squirrels and birds and check on my apricot, pear and apple trees. They were about the only things I enjoyed. There I was, locked in with squirrels, birds, trees and Cadillac cars!

Follow Me!

I thought I was hot stuff. But my heart was empty and my mind was confused. I wasn't happy. I caught myself living in a false world. It was worthless — empty.

My mother's prayers may have had something to do with my unhappiness. She was a great pray-er. She prayed for me and gave me to God, and eventually I couldn't even enjoy wealth!

I got mad at myself for having four Cadillacs. I usually drove the white one. One day, though, I decided to drive a big, fancy green one I had bought from a senator. But it wouldn't start. It had sat so long, the battery had run down. That exasperated me!

While at Georgia Institute of Technology on a business trip, I came to myself. "It's stupid to own four cars," I said. "I don't want to deal with the upkeep. I'd rather have just one or two cars and keep the batteries charged."

So I fell to my knees and prayed, "God, I'm tired of this empty life. Use me! Take me!" Then I stood up and went about my business. I didn't feel any different.

The next week, God manifested Himself to me for the first time. I had driven from Indianapolis to Columbus, Ohio, for an end-of-year business meeting at my manufacturing company. The three of us on the executive board had no problems getting along with each other. We hadn't had even a small spat in more than a year. As far as I was concerned, everything looked perfect.

After the meeting I stepped into my car and started driving down West Broad Street on old U.S. Highway 40 toward Indianapolis. (That was before Interstate 70 was built.)

I started praying a sweet little prayer, thanking Jesus for the day. I didn't know how to pray very well but I could thank the Lord for His blessings. I wasn't thinking about anything very spiritual.

Then, suddenly, it was as if a whirlwind came down from heaven and surrounded my car. And there sat Jesus in the front passenger seat!

I started to weep. I couldn't help myself. Jesus stayed in my car for an hour-and-a-half and I wept the whole time.

As I pulled into the Richmond, Indiana, city limits, that whirlwind of power began to lift off of me. It left the car and I began to come to myself. In a few minutes, I found myself sitting in the driver's seat just as I was before Jesus appeared. God's glorious presence was gone.

But I felt different. Everything about me — my mind, body and heart — felt like I had taken a bath with four bars of soap. I was the cleanest-feeling fellow you could imagine.

My whole body felt healed, right down to my knee-caps, toes and fingertips, and I didn't even know that I needed healing!

The whole time Jesus was with me, I cried. Now, I was a business executive, and I never cried. A business executive tells everybody what to do. He doesn't cry. That is, unless Jesus rides with him in his car.

I thought I was important until Jesus showed up. Then I found out that *He* was the important One.

At least I had enough sense not to mouth off something stupid like, "Now listen, Jesus, I'm an important business executive." I was sitting with the One Who makes worlds! Can you imagine how stupid it would have been for me to tell Him how important I was? To Him, a millionaire business executive has no higher position than his executive suite janitor, glory to God.

When Jesus appeared to me, He changed me. I didn't know He was a killer. He murdered all darkness! He slaughtered all confusion! He killed everything that wasn't joy!

The only message I heard from Jesus during that visit was that He wanted me to follow Him the way His disciples in the New Testament did. *(See* Matthew 4:18-22, 9:9; John 1:43.) I wanted to answer Him, but I couldn't. I was crying so hard, I was gasping for breath!

I wanted to say, "What do You want *me* to follow You for, Lord? I don't have any sense! I thought You called preachers, not businessmen! Why would You want a business executive, Lord? I'm not a preacher. I'm not anything!"

Of course, Jesus already knew all that. That's why He came to me: to straighten out my thinking and make me into something.

After Jesus left peace and joy possessed every ounce of me for the first time since I was a teenager. I even had peace in my eyes! It seemed as if the whole world stopped still before me.

I'm glad nobody saw me crying. I would have been embarrassed. But Jesus had mercy on me and appeared to me while I was alone.

If you want to know the truth about the matter, I thought Jesus must have been pretty hard up. I couldn't figure out what He wanted with me. I had business sense, but I knew I had no spiritual sense. All I knew was that heaven was a good place and God was good. But when Jesus left, I knew two more things. I knew that He loved me and that He wanted me to follow Him. All I had ever done for Him was give a little money to help build the church in my town. And now He wanted me to work for Him!

Putting Jesus First Carries a Price

Jesus' visit was expensive. My wife wouldn't accept it. If you had told me when I left home that morning that my wife and I would ever divorce, I would have called you crazy. I thought my marriage was as solid as the foundation of the county courthouse.

My wife and I had no problems. She kissed me probably fifteen times at the door as I left. She even told me, "Oh, Nohvel, the longer we're married, the more I like to kiss you!" (She was from Boston, and spoke with that accent. She called me "Nohvel.")

"Well, just keep it coming," I would say. She was beautiful and it was easy to kiss her, especially since I loved her.

Nona was a very unusual woman. Have you ever known a person to love somebody so much it was sick? That's about the way she loved me. She wouldn't let me hire a housemaid. "Nohvel," she said, "I want to wash your plate. I get angry when somebody else washes your dishes." She bought me a big living room easy chair. Every day when I came home from work she met me at the door looking like she just stepped out of *Vogue* magazine. She took my hand, led me to the living room and sat me down in that chair.

Then she took my shoes off my feet, put my house shoes on and brought me the newspaper. (I liked to look at the sports page.) She bent down, kissed me two or three times and said, "Just rest here, Honey. I'll call you when dinner's ready."

That's the way my life was every day. I felt like I lived in a castle with a queen.

If somebody pulled a joke on me, she'd get angry and tell them to leave me alone.

"Noni," I'd say, "they don't mean anything by it."

"I don't like it," she'd say. "You're mine and nobody is going to talk to you that way. I'm not going to put up with it."

Part of me felt good about her doting on me. It really was too much. But I didn't care. Are you kidding? I liked the attention.

Our daughter Zona thought I was great, too, and wanted to go with me everywhere. I wasn't any better than any other daddy, but she thought I was.

An Unexpected Response

But as wonderful as my home life was, the Devil was at work trying to steal my destiny. So as I drove home that day after Jesus appeared to me, I was sure my family would be proud. I was sure they would jump up and down with me because God Almighty had visited a human being! But oh brother, was I wrong.

I pulled in the driveway, parked, and walked through the breezeway to the kitchen door.

As I walked in, my wife was standing by the sink. She turned around, looked at me and said, "Nohvel, what's wrong with you? You look like you've seen a ghost!"

"You wouldn't believe it if I told you," I said.

"Told me what?"

"I was driving home in the car," I said, "when Jesus appeared and rode in the front seat with me for an hour-and-a-half!"

"Who?" she said.

"Jesus. You know, God. The One Who made the world. God."

"What did He want?" she asked.

"He wants me to work for Him," I said.

"He wants *you*? What does He want you for?"

"That's what I've been trying to figure out," I said. "I don't know why He wants me, but He does. And I told Him He could have me."

"What?!" my dear, sweet wife shouted.

"He stayed in the car for an hour-and-a-half. He wants me and I told Him, 'yes.'"

"Yes what? What does He want you for?"

"I don't know," I said. "He just wants me."

"Now Nohvel," she said, while shaking her head, "I'm not going to do that. I won't!"

Nona was raised in a socialite family in Boston and New York. And I mean to tell you that socialite demon is a mean one to break. But I didn't know it was a demon. I was ignorant about demons. So were my church and my pastor. How in the world could I know anything about demons?

You may think everybody in your house is all right, but they may not be. If you had told me that my wife had a devil, I'd have told you that you were crazy. Are you kidding?

"You're not going to do what?" I asked.

"I'm not going!" she said.

"What do you mean you're not going? Not going where? I'm not going anywhere!"

"Nohvel Hayes," she said, "I know you. When I married you eleven years ago, you had twenty dollars to your name and your grandmother even gave *that* to you."

"I know it," I said. "I begged you not to marry me. I told you that you were crazy to marry me when I only had twenty dollars."

"I'd have married you if we ate out of tin cans for the rest of our lives," she said. "I married you because I loved you, not because of how much money you had. I've watched you build your corporation up from nothing. Now it's nearly an empire. I helped you a little in the beginning, but you built it up.

"Nohvel," she continued, "you are an unusual man. When you do something, you do it all the way. And I know if you told the Lord that He can have you, you'll probably go to Africa and live in a tent. And I'm not going!"

"What do you mean?" I asked. "I'm not going to Africa and live in a tent!"

"What's wrong with you?" I asked.

"The Lord just called me tonight, and already you have me living in Africa under a tent! I'm not going to do that."

"Yes, you will," she said, "because you're determined. And I'm not going!"

"Well," I said, "If Jesus tells me to go to Africa, I'll go."

"Nohvel," she continued, "I don't want to be around that kind of people all my life."

"What kind of people?" I asked.

"Well, you know, church people," she said. "I was raised in a social world and I live in that world. I have a social life. It's good to go to church on Sunday if you want to, but I'm not giving up my social world, Nohvel, to be a full-time missionary. I'm a social lady, not a missionary."

"Well," I said, "I'll do what Jesus tells me to do."

"Then I'll just get a divorce!" she said.

This really startled me. "What?" I exclaimed. "What did you say?"

"I'll just get a divorce," she said again.

"Jesus came to me and asked me to follow Him, and you want a divorce? Are you crazy?"

"I'll either have all of you for myself, or I won't have any of you!" she said.

"Well then," I said, now angry and confused, "you won't have any of me!"

A Broken Family

We talked all night but nothing changed. And we never again lived as man and wife. She got the divorce and gave me our child.

I told her she shouldn't divorce me. "A woman who treated me the way you did must have loved me," I said. "You're sharp and good-looking. You're sure to marry again. How will you handle living with a man you don't love as much as you did me?"

"Well," she said, "maybe we can get married again, Nohvel."

"Nooo," I said. "I don't want to marry you again. You need to give your life to Jesus right now."

God used to tell me to talk to her about Him.

I'd go see her, and the glory of God would come and shake her as she sat on the couch.

"Fall on your knees and repent," I'd say. "Tell God you'll pass out tracts."

"No, no, no," she'd reply. She wouldn't do it.

Eventually, she moved to San Francisco. After she left, I tried to shake off her memory, but I couldn't. I was still in love with her.

So I wound up by myself, with a broken heart and my nine-year-old daughter, Zona, hanging onto me.

I began to seek the Lord Jesus. I was so hungry for God that I went to every church I could find.

If I saw a revival listed in the newspaper, I went. I would go every night if possible. Sometimes, I asked someone to watch Zona for me. Other times, I took her with me.

The Pain of Divorce

Zona would cry half the night because her family was breaking up. She'd have nightmares. She'd wake up in the middle of the night screaming, "No! No! No! Not my mommy and daddy! No! No! Not our home! No!"

I would grab her and shake her. "Zona, wake up, honey. Wake up! You're screaming. Wake up!"

She'd open her eyes and say, "What, Daddy? What? Oh, Daddy, are you and Mommy really going to break up?"

And I would have to say, "That's the way it is, Honey."

My God, if you're a parent, please don't break up your family for the sake of your children, at least. Your children don't deserve to have their family broken up. The Bible says, ...**and a little child shall lead them** (Isaiah 11:6). That's how God led me, only at the time I didn't know it was God.

My daughter began begging me to move us to Cleveland, Tennessee, where I was raised. Some of her cousins lived there. So I finally agreed. I wasn't going to be guilty of breaking her heart more than it already was broken. Are you kidding? After Jesus showed up in my car, Nona left me, and Zona could have anything she wanted, as far as I was concerned.

So I bought a restaurant there and we moved. We arrived in my hometown on a cold, rainy night. My daughter was so brokenhearted. And I was a bewildered man with the call of God all over me. I was so ignorant of the things of God, I didn't know what to do next. But, step by step, God began to train me.

The first thing He taught me was to love all kinds of people. Sometimes I worked with millionaires. Other times I worked with dirty, smelly people around the city dump.

Then my ex-wife remarried. Have you ever loved your spouse and had them divorce you and marry someone else? I couldn't help letting that control my thoughts nearly every waking minute of every day. I had to wear out my body to fall asleep. Many nights, I'd still be awake at 4 or 5 a.m. That lasted a whole year.

Then I started praying to die. Dear God, I begged Him for more than a year to let me die. That's how raw my life had become. I just wanted to close my eyes and never wake up.

But I had said "yes" to Jesus that day in the car. I had that going for me. The Lord would come and bless me, and I would feel good for two or three days.

A Burden Lifted

Then one day, as I prayed in my office, the Holy Spirit reached deep down inside of me, took hold of all my love for my ex-wife, and in one moment pulled it out of me. I felt like a sock turned wrong side out, as every emotional attachment to my ex-wife was suddenly gone. I was as free as a flying bird, glory to God forever!

You have no idea what a burden lifted off of me! I had lived with that situation twenty-four hours a day for more than a year. All that time I couldn't shake it. I had prayed to die because of it. But then God lifted that burden out of me. Glory to His name forever!

After some time, my ex-wife and I had to meet to settle ownership of a small piece of property. She offered to give me her half for ten thousand dollars, and I agreed.

So I prepared a check for her and we decided to have a meal together. Now, at this time she was married to somebody else, but she didn't know that God had delivered me from loving her. As we sat eating together, she said, "Nohvel, if you tell me not to, I will never go back to California. Never!"

"Oh?" I said. "I guess you're not too happy, huh?"

"Well, Nohvel, I stayed married to you for eleven years. I have more respect for you than any other man I have ever met. I don't treat my new husband as well as I treated you. I would never treat any other man like that, because I love you. I tell my husband what to do twenty-four hours a day. And I feel if he doesn't like it, he can just get out."

"Oh, then you're not really in love with him?" I asked. "How does it feel to be married to someone you're not in love with?"

Nona didn't answer. Instead, she repeated, "I'll never go back to California if you tell me not to."

"What if I don't tell you not to," I said. "What will you do then?"

"Well," she said, "I have a two-year-old son there. I guess I'll go back."

"Then you'll be going back," I said. "You see, I couldn't marry you now, anyway."

"Why not?" she asked, looking surprised and disappointed.

"Because," I said, "I'm not in love with you anymore."

"What!?" she said. That really got to her.

"Look at me," I said. "With you sitting there, as pretty as you are, I have absolutely no desire to kiss you. None."

"My God, Nohvel, don't say that!"

"Well," I said, "I'm saying it, and thank God for it. God is the cause of it. Nona, when I still loved you and you married someone else, I nearly went crazy."

So we settled our business and she went back to California.

And there I was in Tennessee, trying to find my ministry. I had no earthly idea what it was supposed to be.

All I knew to do was pray. That's what the old-fashioned Baptists did when I was a kid.

Finding My Ministry

Jesus told me He wanted me to follow Him, but I didn't know how! How do you follow Him? Do you go to church on Sunday? That's about all I had ever been taught. I didn't know.

But the Lord knew my heart. So one day, as I worked in my restaurant, a minister came in.

"Are you the new owner?" he asked.

"Yes," I said.

"The owner before you sponsored a radio broadcast for our church," he said. "Do you want to do the same?"

I opened my mouth to answer and the Spirit of God shook me and spoke to my heart, "You need to talk to him!"

"Uh, uh, reverend," I stuttered, "do you have a few minutes?"

"Sure," he replied.

"God wants me to talk to you," I explained. "Let's go across the street to my office."

When we got to my office, I poured my heart out and told him my story. "The call of God is on me and I don't know what to do about it," I said. "I don't know what my ministry is. The only thing I can tell you, pastor, is that Jesus loves me and that He wants me to follow Him. But I have no earthly idea what He wants me to do! Can you help me, pastor? Can you tell me what to do?"

Now, what that pastor told me helped me and it will help you, too, if you'll just do it.

"Norvel," he said, "just be faithful to the church."

"Yeah," I responded. "I'm trying. I'm convinced that I go to church more than anybody in town. I go mostly to Baptist churches and revivals, though, because I'm Baptist."

Well wouldn't you know that it just happened to turn out that this pastor was a Pentecostal preacher. I didn't know why God wanted me to talk to him in particular. I didn't know any Pentecostal people. I didn't even know people like him or churches like his existed! (And in those days there weren't very many of them.)

This pastor asked me to come to his church and teach a Sunday school class. And boy were those the meanest little kids I'd ever seen! They kicked each other and squirmed and fought right in class!

In the First Baptist Church, we had some manners. We didn't do that. If I had kicked people in my Sunday school class, my daddy would have nearly killed me.

I had to put some of those Pentecostal kids into another class so I could teach. And that was my first experience leading a Sunday school class.

"Oh, God," I asked, "is this what You want me to do?"

After class, I walked upstairs. I was about to leave and go to my church, but I wanted to be nice to the pastor. So, I sat in the sanctuary where he had already started preaching.

I was sitting there enjoying the sermon — it was the first time I had heard him preach — when all of a sudden a woman to my left said, *"Gor-ka-moko-haya!"* Yeah, that's right — "Gor-ka-moko-haya!"

What was that? I thought. It really grabbed my attention, but nobody else seemed to notice. At the First Baptist Church, you don't break out in saying "Gor-ka-moko-haya!" while the preacher is preaching. You sit there quietly and listen.

Well, this woman didn't say anything else, and I went back to listening to the sermon.

A few minutes later, I was enjoying his preaching when suddenly I heard, *"ROGO-LOMO-LOKOMO!"* It was that woman again!

"What did she say?" I thought.

Then I saw some kind of movement out of the corner of my eye. She did it so quickly, I could just get a glimpse.

What is she doing? Why is she jerking like that? I thought, *I have to see what she's doing!*

I decided to watch her. I looked at the preacher, then I looked at her. (She had kind of a high hairdo.) I thought something had to be wrong with her, but I couldn't figure it out. And now, she was just sitting there as nice as could be.

But I was keeping one eye on the preacher and the other eye on her.

Then, sure enough, in a few minutes I caught her! As I looked at her, she said, *"ROGODO-GORODOR!"*

Oh, God! That stunned my mind! I was an ordinary First Baptist business executive. So I did what any good Baptist would do. I bowed my head.

"Oh, God," I prayed. "Have mercy upon this poor soul who has come here today from the mental institution. Help her, Lord, if it be Thy will. Help her out of those goofy spells."

I have thought about that prayer many times since then. I was as sincere as I could be but I didn't know she was talking in tongues.

If I were God, I would have reached down and mashed my face into the cushion on the pew.

But if God would have told me that night, "She's not from the mental institution, Norvel. She's speaking with other tongues," I would have said, "What? Leave me, Satan!"

And I made up my mind, "When this service is over, I'm going to act like a real nice Baptist and ease on out the door. I don't want to shake hands with anybody, especially that woman! And I won't ever bother these people again, Lord. I promise!"

So, when the service ended, I left.

A few days later, that pastor came to see me. He was just as nice as ever and he acted like nothing had happened that Sunday in his church.

I thought he would apologize to me for that woman's behavior. But he didn't even mention it. Are you kidding? It didn't bother him. And I was a nervous wreck!

New Connections

And praise the name of Jesus forever, that pastor kept in touch with me. Once, he called and said, "Norvel, I want you to go to a Full Gospel Businessmen's Fellowship meeting with me."

"What's that?" I asked.

"A lot of businessmen get together and talk about the Lord."

I wouldn't go, but he kept asking me to come to the meetings.

Then one day, he called and told me that a rich man who owned a certain chain of department stores was going to speak. I was familiar with those stores. I knew they were fancy. *He must have some sense,* I thought.

"He's going to tell his life story," the pastor said.

149

"Yeah," I said, "I might like to hear that."

The truth is, the only reason I went to that meeting was because the speaker was a rich business executive like me. Otherwise, I wouldn't have gone.

I didn't much like how the program began. Those men in that Holiday Inn ballroom started singing, "I don't care what church you belong to...."

Now, I don't know about Methodists, Presbyterians or Catholics, but if you want to turn a Baptist the wrong way, just start singing, "I don't care what church you belong to!"

To a Baptist, brother, you're either Baptist or you're just trying to get there! That's the way it is!

Now every other denomination may be the same way. I don't know about them. But until I was grown, I thought everybody in the world was Baptist.

The next thing I heard was, "Just as long as you're for Jesus you stand!"

Now, I'll go for that part! I thought. *I believe in standing for Jesus. But don't give me that off-the-wall idea, "I don't care what church you belong to." I'm Baptist, and proud of it! I don't want to get involved with any strange people or strange doctrines.*

I knew that place was strange when I walked in. The women weren't wearing any makeup, and there were no ashtrays on the tables. The women I knew in the Baptist church always wore makeup, and we had ashtrays everywhere. In the church I went to, we gave a smoke break just before the Sunday morning service!

Maybe you don't know, but in Tennessee and North Carolina where tobacco is raised, Baptists do smoke. I had smoked cigarettes since I was a kid. My daddy smoked, and my grandpa chewed tobacco. Grandpa used to give me chewing tobacco when I was a little boy. I didn't know it was wrong to use tobacco until I started seeking God.

Then, in that Full Gospel Businessmen's Fellowship meeting, that rich business executive started to give his testimony.

"I have a special chair in my office in the department store," he said. "I can sit there and look out over the shoppers. Sometimes God shows me someone who's dying of cancer."

"My God," I thought. "My mother died of cancer. I wonder if he's telling the truth?"

"I go out to that person," the speaker continued. "I tap them on the shoulder and tell them what the Lord told me. Then I invite them to my office. I ask them to sit in that chair and I lay my hands on them in Jesus' name and pray that they be healed. And the Lord heals them while they're sitting right there!"

Boy, I came alive! I had never seen anyone healed in church, much less in an office!

"But you know," he went on, "I couldn't do things like that until after I was baptized in the Holy Ghost and spoke with other tongues."

As he talked, I looked at one side of his face. Then I leaned over and looked at the other side. After a while, I thought, "He doesn't know what he's talking about. He doesn't have any other tongues. He only has one."

I know you're probably thinking, "Nobody in the world is that dumb." Let me tell you, I was.

Dummy me had never heard anyone talk about speaking in other tongues. So I kept going to Full Gospel

Businessmen's Fellowship meetings. If I hadn't met that Pentecostal preacher, there is no telling where I would be. I might have some kind of ministry, but it would not have been God's divine destiny for me.

New Experiences

What impressed me more than anything else about those precious full-gospel businessmen was that they came from so many different denominations.

After attending their meetings for nearly two years, I heard about an overseas trip they were planning, and my Pentecostal pastor friend urged me to go.

If you never step out and show Jesus that you want to work for Him, you could live and die and never let God show you your ministry. The first missions trip that Full Gospel Businessmen's Fellowship ever took was also my first missions trip. My pastor friend went to Chattanooga with me to have my passport picture taken. Then we all met in New York and flew to England for two weeks to witness in London's hospitals, schools and on the streets. We worked on the streets until after midnight, standing in the rain, trying to get kids saved and off of drugs. It was my first effort to do much for God.

Boy, did I have some experiences!

We pulled a lot of hippies off the street. We got them saved, then sent them up to a certain room in the Hilton Hotel where we were staying. We had hired the hotel barber for twenty-five dollars an hour to cut hair. He just sheared those hippies like sheep! Hair piled ankle-deep all over the floor!

Near that room we reserved another room and filled it with all kinds of food. The hippies didn't have any food.

Most of them were filthy and some of them hadn't slept in a bed for six months. So after we had their hair cut, we sent those hippies to the room where the food was set out. They had to knock on the door and say "Jesus," or they couldn't get in.

Thank God for full-gospel, Pentecostal people. Today I have thousands of the sweetest Pentecostal friends in the world. To get me into my ministry, to ensure my destiny, God sent me to them. You can't learn something from someone who doesn't know anything. You have to meet someone who believes in divine healing before you can learn anything about divine healing.

I had no earthly idea that the Lord's power could work through Christian businessmen.

One day, after we were in London about a week, I was visiting with a Pentecostal businessman in the hotel lobby. As we stood there talking, a little red-haired hippie fellow walked by. He was wearing thick glasses and his eyes were crossed. I didn't know it, but the Holy Spirit was preparing me for my ministry. I was at the right place at the right time.

You can't be at the right place at the right time if you always stay at home. If you want to see the Holy Spirit move, you have to go to where people need help.

This businessman said to me, "The Lord just told me that if we'll go over and pray for that hippie, He will heal his eyes right now. Do you believe that?"

"Sure," I said. "Why not?" I wasn't sure what I believed, but I knew I was *trying* to believe. As long as you're trying, God will help you. As long as you're trying to bloom and get a little sunshine, the Lord will train you over time and help you bloom. So don't cut yourself off from God by staying home unless you're going to a church service.

This businessman walked over to that hippie and said, "Take your glasses off, son." That man was bold. You're bold when you're full of the Holy Ghost. Because when you're full of the Holy Ghost, you can believe God for anything.

I wasn't full of the Holy Ghost, so I let this other businessman do the talking.

"Son," he told the hippie, "God told me that if we prayed for you, He would heal your eyes right now."

The young man took off his glasses. Then that businessman said, "Come on, Brother Hayes. Let's lay hands on him."

I agreed, and we laid hands on him and began to pray. Then the businessman told the Devil what to do and started claiming a miracle for the young man. I followed along, praying like he did. When we finished praying, my businessman friend picked up a paper with print on it. Then he told this hippie, "Now read this without your glasses." I mean, that businessman wasn't afraid of anything!

"Could you read before?" he asked.

"Oh, no," the hippie said. "I couldn't even see the paper without my glasses."

The young man took the paper and started reading aloud, word-for-word.

About then, a fellow with a camera slung over his shoulder walked up.

"Wait a minute!" he said. "I'm a reporter for the *London Herald*," (a newspaper sent worldwide).

He turned to the hippie. "Before they prayed for you, young man," he asked, "could you read that?"

"No," said the young fellow. "I couldn't read anything."

Then we tried an experiment. The hippie could read the paper without his glasses, but when he put those glasses on, he couldn't read it.

The reporter turned to us. "What are your names?" he asked. "Who are you all?"

"We're businessmen from America," my friend said. "There are three jet-loads of us here. We've come to invade London!"

The reporter started writing in his little book. Now get ready for this, glory to God. The next morning the newspaper headline read, in BIG LETTERS, "U.S. Businessmen Come to London; Beatniks Getting Delivered." You can imagine how many millions of people saw that headline. Glory to God!

Now listen, I'm talking about obedience, and ministry, and how they affect your destiny. In two days that hotel was packed. You couldn't get a room. People poured in from all over Europe and we started holding meetings, every day. We had a full-gospel convention, glory to God!

Another Encounter With the Lord

Those kids on the streets of London were so pitiful we just had to help them. We worked so hard for Jesus, standing out in the rain, that a number of us caught colds, myself included. I finally got to feeling bad enough one day, that I decided to stay in my room and pray instead of ministering on the street.

Hotels in foreign countries do things differently than in the United States. The hotel staff sent two nurses to my room. As they walked in, one carried a big, covered pan of hot water. Then they put something in the water, and one of them said, "Come over here, Mr. Hayes. We want you to hold your head over this pan."

"My head? What for?" I asked.

"We put some stuff in this water," one said. "When we take this cover off, the vapors will go right through your nose, unstop everything and make you breathe good."

They uncovered that pan of steaming water and I leaned down over it as they covered my head with a towel. I started breathing in that steam. It felt so good! And my nose opened up! You can learn a lot from old countries.

Every little while they'd bring up another pan of water and repeat the treatment.

So I just stayed in my room, out of the rain. Late that afternoon, something happened that I will never forget. For the first time, God talked to me not by an inward witness but with an audible voice.

As I walked out of my hotel bathroom, God's power hit me and He said to me in a loud voice, "You can't live your life over again! Go get the Bible!"

No one had ever talked to me with that much power. I started weeping, staggered across the room, picked my Bible up off the bed, fell to the floor and started sobbing, crying for mercy.

The room was so full of God's holy presence, I couldn't stand up. The meat on my face felt like it was going to melt onto the Bible. My flesh couldn't stand it. God's presence was so clean, so holy. The Holy Ghost inside me — the Spirit of God — was jumping.

Since then God has spoken to me in an audible voice five or six times. And I want to tell you, if He ever speaks to you that way, it will scare half the life out of you. You won't know what's happening. That's the way it was for me.

Nobody was in the room except God and me. I buried my face in the rug and sobbed, "What do You want, God? What do You want with me? Help me, Jesus! Have mercy on me!"

"You have been raging against Me," God said. Then He quoted the following Scripture to me.

> **Because thy rage against me and thy tumult is come up into mine ears, therefore I will put my hook in thy nose, and my bridle in thy lips, and I will turn thee back by the way by which thou camest.**
>
> **2 Kings 19:28** (See also Isaiah 37:29)

Do you think that's a hard statement? If you do, look at what Jesus said in Luke 12:48:

> **...For unto whomsoever much is given, of him shall be much required....**

God had given me much and He required much of me.

And if you don't believe the Bible, you're raging against God. At the time God spoke to me in England I hadn't completely accepted the idea of speaking with other tongues. And I wondered about many other biblical ideas. I wondered whether casting out devils was for today. I wondered if it was God's will to heal everyone. I was allowing my thoughts to go against God's Word in those areas, and so I was raging against God.

We are each responsible for our own thought life. My mind was so messed up with man-made doctrines that God could hardly do anything with me. And as long as you think like that, you'll be messed up, too. I couldn't have even understood Chapter 3 of this book back then (Doctrines and Gifts). So God started waking me up with an audible voice!

We need to let God be God. We need to trust His Word.

Then God quoted the next verse to me.

And this shall be a sign unto thee, ye shall eat this year such things as grow of themselves, and in the second year that which springeth of the same; and in the third year sow ye, and reap, and plant vineyards, and eat the fruits thereof.

2 Kings 19:29 (Also see Isaiah 37:30)

God was talking to me about my ministry — His destiny for my life.

"This tonight is a sign unto you," He said. "During the first year from now, I want you to let things happen as they will. And during the second year, I want you to let things spring up in your life, even as during the first year. But during the third year from now, I want you to sow seed for Me, and plant vineyards for Me, and you, son, are going to eat the fruit thereof."

To me, sowing seed and planting vineyards meant passing out tracts, witnessing and whatever else I could do for Jesus.

We all eat the fruit from our own vineyards. Then, after God finished speaking to me, all of His holy, clean presence left, and I came to myself. There I was, Norvel

Hayes, lying on the floor of my room in the Hilton in London, England.

That day God gave me a first glimpse of my ministry. He didn't show it all to me at once. And He might not show you all of your ministry at once, because you might not be able to stand it.

When God said to me, "You can't live your life over again," He meant, you can't let past experiences keep you from stepping into God's divine plan for your life. If you do, Satan can use those experiences to steal your destiny. You have to leave the past behind and go on with God.

There in that London hotel room, I hadn't expected God to manifest His presence to me. I wasn't expecting anything like that. But Jesus had called me to follow Him and He saw that I was trying to find my ministry and my destiny in Him. So He came to help me.

I was trying to help people. The Full Gospel business-men taught me some things about that. They believed in missions work. And I did the best I could with what I knew. But I was so ignorant. I could talk to people about getting saved. In all my years of going to church, though no one had ever shown me how to pray for blind people on the street. I hadn't been taught that it was okay to pray shamelessly for people in a hotel lobby. I was never around Christians who did those things. I didn't know people who ministered like that even existed! But I was finding out they existed, I can tell you that!

Some of those businessmen would stop someone on the street and just start talking to them. They'd reach out and touch them and pray for them right there on the sidewalk! They thought no more about it than taking a drink of water!

Oh God, I thought, *I wish I could be that bold. Why am I so bound up?*

I was afraid of what people would think or say. And fear, next to lust, is the most deadly trap the Devil sets. Don't let the Devil steal your destiny through fear. God can teach you how to overcome fear.

God Promises Blessings

For the next seven years I did whatever I could for the Lord, trying to sow seeds and plant vineyards for Him. I taught the Bible, fed the poor, led high school assemblies, worked to get kids off of drugs, raised money to build churches and prayed for everything that moved. And God blessed me while I did that.

Still, after all of that, He told me that I was a flake.

"Oh, really?" I asked.

"That's right," He said. "You're just like many churches. The church is sadly lacking. They don't worship Me enough, and neither do you!"

It was then that God showed me what He would do for churches and individuals who worship Him. He also showed me how important it is to cast out devils, win souls and love beaten-down people.[1]

He told me to spend time in a room by myself, worshiping Him.

"If you obey me, son, and let Me be your God," He said, "I will bless you even more than the prophets of old. I will bless you with such finances that some people in the world will ask you how they came your way."

[1] For a fuller revelation of this read my book, *Worshiping God.*

Then He said, "Son, I'm going to ask you to do something for Me, and I will bless you if you do it. When I promote My servants with position or money, nearly all of them stop casting out devils in My name.

"I'm asking you, son, as long as you are on the earth, to cast out devils. They must obey you as long as you live your life according to My Word."

During those first seven years of ministry, God manifested Himself to me and talked with me in an audible voice three times. He spoke with me like He did the apostle John on the Isle of Patmos (see Revelation 1:10), and the apostle Peter as he prayed on the housetop (see Acts 10:9-16).

At the end of that seven years, the Lord told me, "I want you to teach people the Scriptures, and what I have taught you."

After hearing God's voice, I don't *want* to disobey Him. That's why I send such a strong message for you to have total victory over the Devil. Whatever God asks me to do, I say, "Okay, Lord. I will." And that's what it's going to take in your ministry destiny.

God never called me to preach, so I don't. He called me and anointed me to sit in the office of the teacher. There is a *drive* in me to do it. I *have* to teach. Sometimes I teach for two or three hours. I may not even need to refer to a Bible. The moment I get up to teach, something happens in my belly — in my innermost being. The Holy Spirit lives in there.

I may have no earthly idea what I'm going to say. But I don't worry about that because, when I open my mouth to teach, the Holy Spirit gives me the words. I just walk

161

around relaxed, turn my vocal cords over to Him and let Him do what He wants to do.

As God has led me over the years, He has changed my whole life. I'm a different person from the man Jesus first visited in that car in Indianapolis. I found out that "I" was my main problem. The greatest deliverance you will ever have is to let God deliver you from yourself. Once you do that, the Devil can't steal your destiny.

God has a destiny for you, and the Devil wants to steal it. But God is ever-present to help you keep Satan from doing that. As you take the time to learn God's ways, give your talents to God, learn to resist the Devil and choose to stay humble, God will lead you into your ministry, and destiny forever.

Pray this prayer today and tomorrow call your pastor to find out where you can start your ministry in helping with God's work.

Heavenly Father, I ask You in Jesus' name: show me when I'm wrong, and what I need to change. Show me Your destiny for my life. I don't want to keep going my own selfish way. I know, Father, that I don't please You all the time, but I want to.

I will not let the Devil steal Your destiny for me. I will use the name of Jesus and resist him. I refuse to yield to him.

I yield to You, heavenly Father, and Your plan for me. I commit myself to helping You today, Lord. I commit myself to start.

Thank You, Lord.

Now, let the precious Holy Spirit of God Who lives in you have His way and minister to you.

About the Author

Norvel Hayes is a successful businessman, internationally renown Bible teacher, and founder of several Christian ministries in the U.S. and abroad.

Brother Hayes founded *New Life Bible Church* located in Cleveland, Tennessee, in 1977. New Life Bible Church grew out of the Bible school's chapel services.

Brother Hayes is also founder and President of *New Life Maternity Home*, a ministry dedicated to the spiritual, physical, and financial needs of young girls during pregnancy; *Campus Challenge*, an evangelistic outreach that distributes Christian literature on college campuses across America; *Street Reach*, a ministry dedicated to runaway teens located in Daytona Beach, Florida; and *Children's Home*, an orphanage home and education center located in India.

Known internationally for his dynamic exposition of the Word of God, Brother Hayes spends most of his time teaching and ministering God's deliverance and healing power in churches, college classrooms, conventions, and seminars around the world.

For a complete list of tapes and books
by Norvel Hayes, write:
Norvel Hayes
P.O. Box 1379
Cleveland, TN 37311

Please include your prayer requests
and comments when you write.

To contact Norvel Hayes,
write:

Norvel Hayes
P.O. Box 1379
Cleveland, TN 37311

*Please include your prayer requests
and comments when you write.*

Other Books by Norvel Hayes

Available from your local bookstore.

Harrison House
Tulsa, Oklahoma 74155

Additional copies of this book
are available from your local bookstore.

HARRISON HOUSE
Tulsa, Oklahoma 74153